Making culture accessible

Access, participation and cultural provision in the context of cultural rights in Europe

Annamari Laaksonen
Interarts Agency, Barcelona

Council of Europe Publishing

Cover design: Documents and Publications Production Department (SPDP), Council of Europe
Layout: Ogham/Mourreau

Council of Europe Publishing
F-67075 Strasbourg Cedex
http://book.coe.int

ISBN 978-92-871-6729-3
© Council of Europe, April 2010
Printed at the Council of Europe

Contents

4

Preface

Why should an intergovernmental organisation defending human rights, democracy and the rule of law be looking at cultural participation and access? I strongly believe that these noble objectives cannot be reached without a strong relationship with culture. The values of democracy and human rights and the legal and institutional systems which protect them are cultural products. They cannot endure without an underlying attachment to democracy and human rights within society. And culture – in the sense of arts, creativity and heritage – is a key to maintaining the culture of democracy and human rights. With its close links to the values on which Europe was founded, culture plays a major part in forging a Europe of solidarity and shared standards.

Today, culture is not only recognised for its contribution to the formation of identities and the sense of belonging, for its economic and market impact, but also for its social and educational potential – that is to say, its power to orient co-existence in multicultural and plural societies. Different forms of cultural expression, traditional and contemporary, help interpret social realities that are increasingly marked by globalisation, interdependency and diversity. We actually need a new skill set adequate for the 21st century – a cultural skill set.

Culture's central place in attaining full human development and bringing human rights alive is evident. The Universal Declaration of Human Rights encompasses cultural rights, which invite participation in cultural life in all societies. Such participation fosters the exercise of active citizenship and promotes cohesion. We are dealing with key questions of democracy, when asking about cultural participation: Who participates in whose culture? How can we best make diverse cultural voices heard? How can our participation in culture be secured, and who should defend it?

I invite you wholeheartedly to study the existing legal and policy frameworks in Europe about access to and participation in cultural life, cultural provision and ultimately, cultural rights presented in this volume. It is important to understand what European countries have achieved, intend to do and could ideally envisage doing to enhance participation and access to culture for all, and thereby stimulate creativity, active citizenship and social cohesion of their societies.

We shall never get tired of promoting ever better cultural governance, and celebrating culture as the soul of democracy!

Gabriella Battaini-Dragoni,
Director General of Education, Culture and Heritage, Youth and Sport
Co-ordinator for Intercultural Dialogue and for the Anti-Discrimination Campaign
Council of Europe

5

Introduction

One of the greatest demands which will be placed upon us will be to find ways for people to live together.

Sharon Jeannette & Dick Stanley
"How will we live together?",
Department of Canadian Heritage, 2002

And above all, there is participation. This has to mean the right to participate in society, to be part of the mainstream as well if that is indicated as to maintain one's own cultural base. It implies presence of diverse cultures, communities and individuals in the cultural market places of contemporary society in theatres, museums, public spaces, art galleries, festivals, in the curricula of universities and arts vocational courses, on radio and on television.

Naseem Khan
"The Combination of Many Voices"
International Forum on Cultural Rights and Diversity, Seoul, November 2006

Culture is mostly about sharing, experimenting, feeling, doing and living together. Culture is about the contents of life, understanding and expressing our reality, and our reactions to the world. A Brazilian academic, Teixeira Coelho, calls culture "a long conversation". It conveys values, symbols, beliefs, manners, ideologies, traditions, and ways to define our life and that of others. We can easily lose ourselves in its complexities when trying to explain how it gives colour to our lives and changes with us – even if it also sometimes limits and imposes controls upon us. It is a challenge to try to define culture, to capture it in a box, put it into norms and tame it into regulations. In the same way, it is a challenge to define participation in culture. Who participates in whose culture? How do we access something that we should already be in? How can we make diverse cultural voices heard? How can our participation in culture be secured, what does that participation mean and who should defend it?

Participation in cultural activities, together with access to them, forms the backbone of human rights related to culture. Understanding access and participation in a wider context also enables us to connect culture with other rights such as access to information, freedom of opinion and expression, education, self-determination and association. Minority rights, and the diversity they protect, also define an important part of the cultural life of a society. Having access to different rights and freedoms – to be able to participate, take a stand, have a say, make our voice heard – helps us feel respected; that we matter as people. Culture gives us our sense of being part of a community and therefore ensuring that we are able to participate in it should be given high priority in policy making. Culture helps us cope, as a Catalan scientist, Eduard Punset, says, with the biggest challenge in life: the contact with another human being. It is about relationships with people, feeling part of and distinct from them at the same time.

Culture not only contributes to the formation of identities and the sense of belonging, it also reflects the forms of co-existence and the construction of symbolic references in multicultural and plural societies. While culture has increased its importance and presence in economic terms and in relation to the market, it has also manifested itself as an important element of social and economic transformation, social cohesion and education for civic democratic participation. Furthermore, nowadays cultural operators are expected to take a stand and to offer new solutions to a wide range of social problems – even if we have to remind politicians that culture cannot be treated as a "supermarket" for easy answers. Cultural policies need to take these factors into account. They must consider all the different dimensions that culture has in people's lives, and promote enjoyment and joy of the arts along with the huge range of human expression.

When we go to a new place or a new country, we want to learn about it – discover the history, visit interesting sites, eat something "local", and bring home something typical. This makes us feel for a moment that we have witnessed and participated in something new and different, a different culture from our own. But when we live in a place we do not always recognise the ways in which we participate in our own culture or understand how to gain access to it. Access is almost always a precursor to participation and we might not even be aware of the channels that exist to make everyone part of cultural experience. It would be ideal if we could have strong cultural experiences where we live in the same way we do when we are not at home, and look at the world with curious eyes. It would be ideal if culture were inclusive and cohesive, accepting, free of discrimination and respectful towards other cultures. It would be ideal if we could feel culturally at home and culturally accepted where we live and when we go to other places. It would be ideal if the policies that regulate and shape our cultural opportunities would take all that into account. Sometimes, though, all it takes to make a difference is an attitude.

There is growing recognition of the influence that culture has on the quality of life and social cohesion. Former French Minister of Culture Jacques Duhamel indicated that culture is not a principle of good governance but a "possibility of common exchange, search and enjoyment". Since the second half of the last century, a realisation of the importance of the right of access to and participation in cultural life has slowly penetrated the field of cultural policies and political discourse, if still only in a marginal and somewhat sporadic way. There is a consensus that culture generates rights and responsibilities and there is a large number of international documents that try to respond to this task. The task becomes more complicated when legal frameworks are translated into policies and action. As always, the transition from theory to practice is a challenging move. As much as we need a strong conceptual and legal basis to facilitate understanding, promotion and protection of certain ideals, the real test is in daily life where we have to face these issues and need to find ways to fulfil promises, resolve problems and maintain a harmonious and enabling environment for interaction.

John Foote (2006) says that "Culture and citizenship require the application of inclusive and legal principles and analysis to the promotion and implementation of cultural, social and economic objectives and policies." Cultural activity, since it promotes creativity, self-expression and self-confidence, should be a key consideration in all forms of social and development policy. Cultural inclusion, when applied to policies on education, civil society and urban design, can strengthen social cohesion. Only by placing values at the heart of the cultural space can policy makers link political concerns with these other policy areas.

Countries resolve issues related to access and participation in different ways but mostly with the same objective; to make culture accepting, inclusive and accessible to everyone. Culture may not always hold a dominant position in the political hierarchy, but equal access and participation are key elements in human dignity, and an enabling environment for a fulfilled life and equal opportunities should be an important concern of states. Countries have a different understanding of culture – or a different understanding of which dimensions of culture need to be secured, protected and fulfilled – but most governments sign up to the contemporary notion that culture is much more than art.

Cultural rights activists often claim that state administrations do not have an interest in cultural rights or the protection of cultural expression. This perception is not wholly accurate, for some states do occasionally manifest interest in the theme. However, their discourses on the subject often cover different areas. The cultural rights discourse is easily submerged under issues with a higher recognised priority. Where cultural activists are correct is that states rarely give culture the budgetary importance its advocates call for.

This study is a general overview of existing legal and policy frameworks in Europe covering access to and participation in cultural life, cultural provision and as a base for cultural rights. It examines what countries in Europe have done, intend to do and could do in the future. It is not an exhaustive study of everything that has been accomplished but a general snapshot of the European situation. The objective is to facilitate an environment that enables the development of access and participation. Bearing in mind that an important part of this work is delivered through local civil society organisations and cultural associations, the study pays tribute to them but does not map out the whole field.

The main thesis of this study is that the enjoyment and fulfilment of the right to participate in culture requires an enabling environment and a legal framework that offers a solid basis for the protection of rights related to cultural actions. It asserts that a society that demonstrates an interest in nurturing cultural and spiritual needs in conditions of liberty – where people have the right of access to cultural expression, experiences, equipment and services has a greater chance of developing a sense of social responsibility among its members.

The author would like to thank Jordi Baltà, Tullia Canale, Maria Giovanna Fara, Mercedes Giovinazzo, Ingrid Hemström, Ourania Kokkinou, Paraic McQuaid, Vassiliki Papakostopoulou, Jose Rey, Uta Staiger and especially Emilie Vidal for their valuable comments and contributions. The study would not have been possible without the editing skills of Simon Mundy and the guidance of Kathrin Merkle.

1. An introduction to the concepts

To try to capture the concept of culture in all its rich variety might sometimes seem a forlorn hope since cultural experience is also about feelings and emotions, and interpreting its different phenomena can easily lead to misunderstandings. But concepts do give us a map to help us navigate, and even if the following concepts might be understood quite differently in diverse settings, they offer general guidelines on how to approach many relevant aspects.

"Cultural democracy" fosters the idea that every person, every community and every cultural minority has cultural requirements and should have certain rights that ought to be respected. It includes the promotion of cultural diversity and active participation in cultural life, together with the facilitation of access to decision-making processes, and to securing equal access to resources and cultural services.

Webster's World of Cultural Democracy defines the concept of cultural democracy as comprising a set of related commitments:

- protecting and promoting cultural diversity, and the right to culture for everyone in our society and around the world;
- encouraging active participation in community cultural life;
- enabling people to participate in policy decisions that affect the quality of our cultural lives; and
- assuring fair and equitable access to cultural resources and support.

In addition, the four principles of the transversal study by Tony Bennett on the subject of policies and cultural diversity ("Differing diversities" for the Council of Europe, 2001) include: the equal right of everyone to participate in the cultural activities of a society; the possibility for all members of a society to benefit from its cultural offer and means without losing their own cultural identity; the obligation of a state to support cultural diversity within society and the promotion of diversity through contact with other cultures.

The Human Development Report 2004, *Cultural liberty in today's diverse world*, underlines the importance of democracy in fostering and implementing cultural rights. "Democracy is the only form of government consistent with all human freedoms and human rights, including cultural freedoms and rights." However, the report also acknowledges that democracy is not impermeable and can have negative results and give space to those who infringe cultural rights and freedoms when extremists are elected. "Democracy does little to accommodate minority interests. Well-developed democracies have neglected claims for cultural recognition from ethnic, linguistic and religious groups, including indigenous groups and immigrants. Democracy also permits the rise of extremist groups."

"Cultural development" promotes social action through culture as a basis for development. It aims to contribute to, for example, the formation of human capital, the cohesion of the social fabric, the strengthening of governance and the cultural integration of a region. The World Conference on Cultural Policies (MONDIACULT, Mexico, 1982) officially established the relationship between culture and development. Other standard-setting instruments include the reports of the World Commission on Culture and Development (1995) and the Intergovernmental Conference on Cultural Policies for Development (Stockholm, 1998); together with many other (mainly UNESCO) documents. According to *Our creative diversity*, the report of the World Commission on Culture and Development in 1995, culture forms the basis of development, and all management and planning of public policies on development should take into account the cultural dimension. When the production-oriented model of development was not delivering the desired results despite the proposals set out in *Our creative diversity* (and other reports such as *In from the margins: a contribution to the debate on culture and development in Europe*, Council of Europe, 1997), many international development organisations started to include elements of cultural development and to foster cultural aspects in their education, social, environmental and economic strategies. At the same time as culture has increased its importance in economic terms and in relation to the market, culture has shown itself to be an important element of social transformation, social cohesion and productive growth. However, culture is still too often left on the sidelines of development thinking, as became clear when cultural aspects were not included in the Millennium Development Goals of the United Nations.

"Cultural diversity": since the early 1990s, the notion of diversity has gained unprecedented importance, thanks to demographic trends, migration and emerging tensions between different population groups. At the same time, an approach that fosters individuals' needs and abilities has gained political ground. It has been stated that diversity empowers everyone to develop to the maximum of their potential and inclination, and is the common heritage of humanity. The Universal Declaration on Cultural Diversity of UNESCO (2001) states in its Article 1: "Diversity is embodied in the uniqueness and plurality of the identities of the groups and societies making up humankind. As a source of exchange, innovation and creativity, cultural diversity is as necessary for mankind as biodiversity is for nature. In this sense, it is the common heritage of humanity that should be recognized and affirmed for the benefit of present and future generations." Cultural diversity is above all a concept that has flourished in the framework of UNESCO. A report published by UNESCO in 2000 shows the development of the concept within the organisation during the second half of the 20th century.[1]

Diversity, of course, means different things in different settings. Naseem Khan (2006) points to the fact that "the British experience differs from the French that differs from the Bulgarian that differs from the Malaysian. However, similar pressures do pertain and the questions themselves cannot be brushed aside". The International Network on Cultural Diversity underlines the importance of cultural diversity as the recognition of cultural plurality within, between and across societies.

The main legal instrument as regards cultural diversity is the Convention on the Protection and Promotion of the Diversity of Cultural Expressions, adopted by the General Conference of UNESCO on 21 October 2005. At the policy level, cultural diversity is understood in various ways and diversity takes many different forms.

"Cultural liberty" means the opportunities a person has to choose his or her way of living without being discriminated against as a result of that choice. Cultural liberty has also been understood at times as the intersection of the concepts of cultural rights and cultural diversity. According to the Human Development Report 2004, around one in every seven people in the world do not enjoy cultural freedom.

"Human rights" have their base in the 30 articles of the Universal Declaration of Human Rights, which was enshrined in international law in 1948. Even if the declaration was not the first international instrument to articulate human rights, it is the central document that asserts their universality. Human rights identify certain objectives and obligations as a common frame for human action. Violations of these rights often have cultural implications – and, indeed, causes. Human rights depend on legislation, policies, resources, diplomacy, relations, reciprocity, participation and education, among other elements. The fundamental

1. "UNESCO and the issue of cultural diversity. Review and strategy, 1946-2000".

instruments of human rights are the Universal Declaration of Human Rights (United Nations, 1948), the International Covenant on Civil and Political Rights (United Nations, 1966 with its two additional protocols) and the International Covenant on Economic, Social and Cultural Rights (United Nations, 1966). Within the structure of the United Nations there are also other instruments that deal with racial discrimination (1965), elimination of all forms of discrimination against women (1979), the fight against torture (1984) and the rights of the child (1989). At the European level the reference document is the European Convention on Human Rights (1950) of the Council of Europe.

A "national minority" is a group of people that live in a region of a country and are citizens of that country. They maintain contact with the state, but at the same time share common ethnic, cultural, religious and linguistic characteristics that are different from those who are considered to be in the majority. They form a sizeable group and share a motivation to maintain their own identity and culture, tradition, religion and language.

14

2. Building access, promoting participation and securing provision

In a liberal democracy, by definition, we want citizens as a whole to determine what are appropriate behaviours, actions and choices to make, because citizens as a whole are the only source of legitimate power to make those kinds of decisions (regardless of the sorts of institutions they have agreed to set up to actually effect the decisions). Exclusion from this determination process (cultural participation) therefore constitutes a failure of democracy. We want every citizen to have an equal right and capacity to influence the interpretation and creation of meaning and all of them to feel ownership. In this way, they are not only empowered and socially cohesive (i.e., willing to cooperate with each other), but also attached to the partnership that is the state. Therefore, all of them must have full cultural access to be complete citizens.

Stanley 2007

The ethical dimensions of cultural policies began to play a more significant role in the 1960s and 1970s when concepts such as cultural democracy and the democratisation of culture were introduced into cultural policy planning. The idea of democratisation of culture fostered everyone's right to participate actively in cultural life. These ideas were supported by the community arts movement (participatory arts) and other social movements that underlined the role culture plays in people's lives. These movements also acknowledged the creative potential that everyone carries within them. After a shift towards the recognition of the economic importance of culture, and culture as a tool for economic development, in the 1980s these ideas were accompanied by ideas of cultural development, cultural citizenship and, subsequently, cultural diversity. Along with these ideas, the concepts of universal participation and of involving people in cultural decision-making processes were gaining ground and started to become key words in policy thinking. These acknowledged the role of culture as a fundamental factor in such social processes as cohesion, cultural citizenship and social and cultural capital.

In recent years, there has been more interest in the impact that access to and participation in cultural activities may have. This is partly due to the fact that the whole idea of culture is much more dynamic and less static than before. The understanding of culture as a capacity-builder or the "sentimental home" of our sense of belonging has increased the interest of policy makers in finding new ways to respond to the needs of individuals and distinctive groups. François Matarasso, for example, found in a European comparative study that participation in cultural activities seemed to have a positive impact on personal development and social capacities. Even though not all forms of participation are uniformly positive, the overall balance is understood to be beneficial (Matarasso 1997).

Fintan O'Toole (writing in 2006) said that participation in cultural life equals full enjoyment of what it means to be human, and exclusion means dropping out of the community and from the full sense of being a human. The Human Development Report 2004 backs this up by saying that when people or groups are not allowed to take part in society, it is called participation exclusion. This is closely linked to the idea of cultural liberty as a fundamental aspect of cultural rights. O'Toole also refers to the report of the National Endowment for the Arts in the United States that relates participation in culture (and in its arts components) and participation in public life. This means that people who participate in cultural life not only have a stronger sense of responsibility towards the community but tend to be more active in it. Those who feel that through their participation in cultural life their sense of being a human is fulfilled and respected also have a stronger sense of social cohesion and of commitment towards the community.

Without the right to participate in cultural life, individuals fail to develop the social and cultural connections that are important to maintaining satisfactory conditions of equality. When people are excluded from cultural life, this can have consequences for the well-being and even sustainability of the social order. Participation in cultural life is closely linked to citizens' ability to build a sense of responsibility in areas such as respect for others, non-discrimination, equality, social justice, the preservation of diversity and heritage, and curiosity for other cultures.

> *In looking at culture in its broadest sense it seems to me to bring up quite a profound question –*
> *because if culture includes all of the creations of humanity, if it includes this continuation of the*
> *process of human exploration and development, then exclusion from culture is not exclusively about*

the fact that you don't get to go to the theatre or the movies, its about something much more profound than that. It's about exclusion from full participation in what it means to be human.

O'Toole 2006

2.1 Access and participation in cultural life

Is cultural participation a basic building block of cultural citizenship, or a way to measure it?

Catherine Murray
from *"Accounting for Culture – Thinking Through Cultural Citizenship"* 2005

The relationship between culture and human rights has created a cultural diversity momentum and is generating a new paradigm, whereby the participation of the citizenry and the implementation and evaluation of policies is no longer an option, but a characteristic of democracy.

Jordi Pascual i Ruiz
from *"Guide to Citizen Participation in Local Cultural Policy Development for European Cities"*, 2007

Access is often described as a fundamental condition for people to participate in society as members with full rights and responsibilities. It is a concept linked to inclusion, representation and promotion of citizenship. Access to cultural services and expressions has slowly converted into the rationale of most cultural policies.

The policy guidelines of the Civil Society Platform on Access to Culture (2009) that forms part of the structured dialogue between the European Commission and the cultural sector describe access to culture as a effective tool to achieve sustainable development in Europe and to bring Europeans together. In the document, access to culture is described as "an essential right of all citizens" that becomes crucial in the case of people in disadvantaged situations. The document reminds us that "only with universal access are a variety of cultural expressions available and thus options for people to freely choose from".

Participation is fundamentally linked to access. Defining participation in cultural life not only depends on how participation is viewed, but also on how cultural life itself is understood. Usually, when participation is discussed in relation to culture the immediate response is that people mostly participate by attending events or using cultural services and programmes. But participation in cultural life can also be understood as being able to have a say in decision-making processes, expressing an opinion, using creative self-expression or enjoying diverse cultural experiences. Participation in cultural life contributes to equality of opportunity. It enables people to associate with a particular community and to contribute to the design and formulation of policies for it.

The consensus is that someone who participates in culture is defined as anyone who attends a cultural activity (for example, attends a concert or takes part in a creative writing workshop) or engages in some other way – by reading a book, speaking a second language, visiting a cultural monument or watching a film. Even having Internet access and using it can be seen as participation in cultural life. This is seen to benefit and empower self-confidence, an important factor in leading a fulfilled life. Studies show that children who have been involved in cultural activities develop a greater consciousness towards other people. Being able to realise their creativity leads to greater assertiveness.

The concept of participation is changing through the use of new technologies. John Holden (2007) has argued that accessing cultural activities through the Internet adds to the democratisation of culture, engages the public in shaping the nature of cultural provision and allows people to contribute to and shape culture for themselves. New technologies might also make access to and participation in cultural life possible for people who are harder to reach through traditional means, or who do not have the same physical opportunities for participation.

In today's cultural policy planning it is easy to establish the objective of making culture as accessible as possible. However, it is harder to pin down exactly what that access entails. Does it mean merely entering a cultural space or having the means to enjoy cultural experiences? How can participation be measured? Who is participating, how and in what?

According to the UNESCO Recommendation on Participation by the People at Large in Cultural Life and Their Contribution to It (1976) access to culture means "the concrete opportunities available to everyone, in particular through the creation of appropriate socio-economic conditions, for freely obtaining information, training, knowledge and understanding, and for enjoying cultural values and cultural property". Participation is seen as "the concrete opportunities guaranteed for all – groups and individuals – to express themselves freely, to communicate, act, and engage in creative activities with a view to the full development of their personalities, a harmonious life and cultural progress of society".

When the United Nations Committee on Economic, Social and Cultural Rights gave a green light to the continuing process of formulating a general comment (enlargement and more detailed definition by 2010 at the earliest) on the right to participate in cultural life (Article 15 (1) (a) of the International Covenant on Economic, Social and Cultural Rights) two of the first questions it asked were what is meant by participation and what is meant by cultural life? It also queried who participates in whose culture?

According to Wikipedia, participation is (in addition to its dictionary definition) divided into the following categories:

- participation (decision making), a notion in the theory of management, economics and politics;
- participation (VR), a notion from virtual reality;
- participation (ownership), sharing something in common with others;
- participation (joining), joining with others in activities;
- participation (finance), getting some benefit from the performance of a certain underlying asset.

Even if these elements refer to participation in general, they can also be adapted to the field of cultural policies. Participation in decision making reflects the idea of cultural democracy. As Jordi Pascual i Ruiz (2007) states "the involvement of citizenry and civil society in policy-making has grown during the last two decades. Unilateral policies are disappearing. The participation of the citizenry in elaborating, implementing and evaluating policies is no longer an option, but a characteristic of advanced democracies. The existence of a strong civil society is the very backbone of democracy and it is marked by a concern of human solidarity."

In 1997 the Statistical Programme Committee of the European Union established an experts' group to study the harmonisation of statistical practices in different countries (Schuster 2007). The committee concluded that "Do we think it essential that cultural participation be defined as a conscious act, with a conscious aim for those who participate? If this is essential, the participator should have a role in defining whether something he/she is doing is 'cultural participation'. Or is the concept defined by somebody else – researcher, cultural politician, etc. – definition being in this sense a cultural policy act?" Mark Schuster pointed out, however, that most participation studies are fairly practical in their approach – concentrating their efforts on measuring: "participation [is] all the ways in which people engage with the particular art forms or cultural activities that are of interest to whomever has commissioned the study". He also points out the distinction between attendance and participation, as well as receptive participation and active participation.

Participation is closely linked to social cohesion. Access and participation are crucial elements of cultural rights and their translation into policies. If that is the case then such policies should not be designed or implemented without the participation of those whom they are going to effect. Individuals should be entitled to choose whether or not they take part in the cultural life of the community. Equally, access to and participation in cultural life forms an essential part of making social policies successful.

Participation in cultural life has been described as a universe of opportunities for people to operate simultaneously in different cultural climates and discourses. It is not meant to lead to the isolation of cultural groups, but rather to a guarantee of equal opportunities for everyone. Cultural participation is also closely linked with cultural inclusion, a term which is related to elements of education, civil society, urban design,[2] mutual knowledge and contributions to policy-making processes. Culture has a strong impact on the construction of social cohesion and how people relate to each other in a society or in a community. Participation, however, varies with its context – from urban to rural and from one cultural environment to another.

In 1998, the Urban Institute in Washington DC conducted a survey on cultural participation. According to that survey cultural participation contributes to cultural and community life through four different forms. Even if the matrix displays participation in culture more in terms of art than culture as an environment, it does give some useful ideas about the importance of participation in cultural life. The findings of the study suggest that active participation in art activities/culture promotes participation in other ways as well, and that participation strengthens commitment towards the community or society itself:

2. Urban design concerns the arrangement, appearance and functionality of towns and cities, and in particular the shaping and uses of safe public space.

Types of arts and cultural participation	Contribution to arts and culture	Contribution to community life
Attendance at life programmes or events	Strengthens arts and cultural institutions by maintaining and expanding their audiences	Sustains and increases connections among people. Contributes to economic development of business districts and neighbourhoods. Supports vitality of community spaces, including schools and places of worship
Amateur art-making (in private, for family or friends, or in public)	Deepens personal understanding of art and cultural forms. Creates opportunities for others to experience arts and culture. Supports arts groups that rely on unpaid performers	Provides shared cultural experiences among family, friends, neighbours, and others that strengthen social ties. Helps preserve cultural practices specific to ethnic groups or regions
Socialisation of children (taking them to events or arranging lessons outside school)	Encourages development of skills and habits of cultural participation. Builds appreciation of arts and cultural experiences, leading to long-term audience building and fostering of support	Encourages children and youth to participate in community-sanctioned activities. Builds personal and social skills. Fosters habits of participation that may carry over to other aspects of community and civic life
Support for artists or arts organisations (through financial contributions or volunteer activities)	Builds the capacity of arts and cultural organisations to offer varied, high-quality programmes. Creates opportunities for people to experience arts and culture	Strengthens the ability of arts organisations to engage in education and community outreach. Supports major institutions that are sources of community pride. Helps community-based organisations that rely on arts and cultural programmes for member services, social programming and fund-raising

The Canadian study on the social effect of culture, published in early 2008 and funded by the Canadian Council for the Arts, the Department of Canadian Heritage and the Ontario Arts Council, shows that, in general, participation in cultural activities enables people to develop a stronger sense of social engagement. François Matarasso's study also indicates that participation in arts activities strengthens people's sense of belonging and that participation helps people to develop useful skills, ranging from communication to creative thinking.

In the introduction to *Guide to Citizen Participation in Local Cultural Policy Development for European Cities* (2007), Philipp Dietachmair refers to the fact that participation is in the end a shared feature of a society:

> *A vibrant, diverse and inspiring cultural life, to which citizens of all local communities and subcultures have access and connect with, makes up a substantial part of the social fabric that determines functioning and attractive living localities and the quality of life that a place offers. What makes an individual a citizen (or not) of a particular town or place is largely determined by cultural aspects.*

2.2 Participation in the context of human/cultural rights

> *Cultural rights are an integral part of human rights, which are universal, indivisible and interdependent. The flourishing of creative diversity requires the full implementation of cultural rights as defined in Article 27 of the Universal Declaration of Human Rights and in Articles 13 and 15 of the International Covenant on Economic, Social and Cultural Rights. All persons should therefore be able to express themselves and to create and disseminate their work in the language of their choice, and particularly in their mother tongue; all persons should be entitled to quality education and training that fully respect their cultural identity; and all persons have the right to participate in the cultural life of their choice and conduct own cultural practices, subject to respect for human rights and fundamental freedoms.*

Article 5, UNESCO Universal Declaration on Cultural Diversity, 2001

> *Rights are central to participation in cultural life and allow individuals and groups of people to follow, adopt or create a way of life of their choice.*

Hansen

"The right to take part in cultural life: towards minimum core obligations related to Article 15 (1) (a) of the International Covenant on Economic, Social and Cultural Rights", 2001

Access to, and participation in, cultural life is mentioned in several international instruments. Participation in cultural life was formulated for the first time in Article 27 of the 1948 Universal Declaration of Human Rights and has since then been reiterated in various forms. The right to participate in cultural life (Article 27) forms the basis of any later development of cultural participation rights as seen in the context of cultural rights. Cultural rights are human rights related to culture, which makes them different from, though often enacted through, cultural legislation. And as human rights aim at assuring human dignity, equality and non-discrimination, cultural rights share the same objectives together with the idea of the protection of the full enjoyment of culture.

When in a recent study respondents were asked what they understood by cultural rights, the answer usually referred to the will to protect a community's way of life – above all the right to use their own language. Kim Su-Kab (2006) states that the term "cultural rights" refers to the "right or benefit of free performance, enjoyment, and succession of culture and cultural heritage, as well as the right to live in a good cultural environment". He groups cultural rights into four categories: cultural freedoms, cultural equity, cultural participation rights and cultural environment rights.

In contrast to other human rights that seek equal treatment for all, cultural rights foster the richness of difference. Stephen Marks (2003) says that "while other human rights are essential to human survival, to bodily integrity, and to material existence, cultural rights are much more than accessory rights. It is not an exaggeration to say that cultural rights guarantee to individuals and to culturally defined groups their sense of meaning. They merit much more attention than they have received, for they are in a real sense the grounding of the aesthetic, cognitive, spiritual and emotional bonds of all humans to their society and the cosmos and their means of expressing those bonds." Minority rights expert Asbjørn Eide has underlined that the right to participate in cultural life can protect people from different threats such as authoritarian governments and that this right has a close link to other freedoms, for example freedom of opinion, expression and information.

Gonzalo Carámbula (2004) says that cultural rights should be shown to cover the relationships of people sharing the same social space rather than the legalities of cultural authority. In other words, cultural rights are tools for redefining the relationships between different groups within the society and the community, not only from the legal point of view, but also from the point of view of experiences that take into account the practicalities of equality. Cultural rights need to be sustained at local and regional levels, where the perception and specific characteristics of local culture may have an impact on their implementation – taking into account the core values of personal freedom.

Cultural rights as we know them have their roots in the Age of Enlightenment and the idea of fundamental freedoms such as freedom of opinion and freedom of expression. According to Franco Bianchini (2005), the concept "cultural rights" comes from the work of a British sociologist in the 1940s that connected the idea of cultural rights with the "cultural competence" of citizens, which included the free exercise of rights, choices and use of opportunities. Cultural rights entered the sphere of international public law in the second half of the 20th century as a result of the Universal Declaration of Human Rights.

Catherine Murray (2003) indicates that when adopting a cultural rights/citizenship model the notion of equality becomes central to the different dimensions of cultural participation. According to her, the right to participate in cultural life has different meanings:

- expressive: implying that people have a basic right to tell stories in their own language or to practice everyday life in different ways, to create and disseminate their work in the language of their choice (Article 1, UNESCO Universal Declaration on Cultural Diversity);
- normative: referring to the civil values of treatment with respect, tolerance, or establishing the security of being, that is the right to live in freedom from fear of arbitrary cultural genocide (preamble, ibid.);
- instrumental: compelling the state to provide the informational tools, education, or identity. Conversely, the state may guarantee access to cultural resources to all, regardless of income or geographic location;
- procedural: including grounds for protection of minorities as an ethical imperative, inseparable from respect for human dignity. It implies a commitment to human rights and fundamental freedoms, in particular the rights of those who belong to minorities and indigenous peoples;
- deliberative: that is, setting out the principles of recognition of cultural status, representation in cultural decision making, or control over cultural self-determination.

In Helsinki in 1992 the Council of Europe held – together with the CIRCLE Network (Cultural Information and Research Centres Liaison in Europe) and the Arts Council of Finland – one of the first seminars on the intersection between cultural rights and cultural policies. The round table observations included a call for a "fresh consideration" of cultural rights and a call for societies and countries to promote participation in cultural life in order to avoid becoming impoverished societies.

As regards access, Absjørn Eide (2002) argues that "cultural rights should give priority to the access to the culture of one's own and to the learning of it as well as to the right to participate in the reproduction and subsequent development of that culture. The individual as a producer of culture becomes important when he/she sees that some of the old traditions are unacceptable or insufficient (in comparison with other practices in other parts of the world). As some of the old traditions may not go along the lines of equality, liberty and personal integrity, the right to innovate and change old habits must also be secured."

In a shared cultural space access to and participation in cultural life forms an essential part of making policies successful. The assertion of cultural rights fosters collective action and can prove to be a powerful instrument. Collective action can contribute to the promotion, defence and protection of cultural rights and awareness-raising. Rudder (2006) believes that "the right to access to the products of other cultures as well as the right of access to one's own culture is therefore fundamental to the acceptance of meaningful cultural diversity".

We are almost at the point when it seems inappropriate to talk about cultural rights as a group. Instead, we should be concentrating on individual rights – such as the right to participate in cultural life or what would be the right to access culture – and their applications.

The cultural rights debate takes different forms in different places. Whilst in Europe and the Western world, the most legally developed areas of cultural rights are related to intellectual property rights and education; outside Europe, cultural rights are often linked to major social themes such as sexual and reproductive rights, mobility and migration. Cultural rights, including the right to participate in cultural life, are individual rights with a collective nature. Yvonne Donders (2004b) underlines this when she states: "Communities are an important factor in creating a valuable life for individuals, and these communities should be protected by collective rights." Simon Mundy (2000) says that "in the global context cultural rights are therefore at the heart of political debate. They can shape the reform of societies, define how communities respond to new arrivals, and underscore the need to balance collective protectionist instincts with a firm defence of each individual's human right not to be coerced by collective pressure."

2.3 Participation in cultural life in the international legal and institutional framework

A cultural framework provides a human being with a sense of meaning, and this meaning is essential to a person's sense of dignity. When human rights protect a person's culture, they are supporting this sense of dignity. In this very fundamental way, culture and human rights complement one another. In addition, specific cultural institutions and practices may be essential to the enjoyment of human rights.

The Banyan tree paradox: Culture and human rights activism, 2006

Cultural human rights are essential to protect an important part of human dignity.

Donders
"The legal framework of the right to take part in cultural life", 2004

Human rights are a system of norms that help to identify goals and obligations as a commonly agreed framework for human action. Universal human rights were embodied in 1948 in international law through the articles of the Universal Declaration of Human Rights. The universal declaration recognises, in Article 27, the right to take part in cultural life. It is from this article, therefore, that the right to participate in cultural life as a human right takes its basis in international law.

In October 2009, the United Nations Human Rights Council appointed the first Independent Expert on Cultural Rights.[3] Within the United Nations system, the independent experts or special rapporteurs are all

---

3. The appointed expert is Ms Farida Shaheed, Pakistan.

called upon to examine, monitor and create UN reports on different rights.[4] The work of the independent expert will be based on international standard-setting instruments. The essential building block of these instruments, Article 27 of the Universal Declaration of Human Rights, stipulates:

1. Everyone has the right to freely participate in the cultural life of the community, to enjoy the arts and to share in scientific advancement and its benefits.

2. Everyone has the right to the protection of the moral and material interests resulting from any scientific, literary or artistic production of which he is the author.

The right to participate in cultural life is also recognised in other instruments of the International Bill of Human Rights,[5] namely Article 27 of the International Covenant on Civil and Political Rights, and Article 15 of the International Covenant on Economic, Social and Cultural Rights, both from 1966. In addition, the UN Committee on Economic, Social and Cultural Rights adopted on 20 November 2009 at its 43rd session general comment No. 21 on the right of everyone to take part in cultural life. The general comment is annexed to this study.

Donders (2002) explains that the first draft of Article 27 of the Universal Declaration of Human Rights did not originally include a reference to culture, only to science, and that it was the United States delegation that proposed the reference to culture as an important aspect of human life, with several countries following –

27

---

4. The Independent Expert on Cultural Rights will be responsible for different actions:
– identifying the best practices in the promotion of cultural rights at the local, national, regional and international levels;
– identifying possible obstacles to the promotion and protection of cultural rights and to submit proposals and/or recommendations to the Human Rights Council for possible actions in that regard;
– working in co-operation with states in order to foster the adoption of measures at the local, regional, and international levels aimed at the promotion and protection of cultural rights through concrete proposals enhancing sub-regional, regional, and international co-operation in that regard;
– studying the relation between cultural rights and cultural diversity, in close collaboration with states and other relevant actors, including in particular UNESCO, with the aim of further promotion of cultural rights.
The creation of the mandate has raised some concerns among activists and organisations working in the field of human rights and especially women's rights, and other marginalised groups.

5. The International Bill of Human Rights consists of five instruments: the Universal Declaration of Human Rights (1948); International Covenant on Civil and Political Rights (ICCPR, 1966); International Covenant on Economic, Social and Cultural Rights (1966); Optional Protocol to the ICCPR and Second Optional Protocol to the ICCPR.

including the Peruvian delegation, who proposed the term "freely" before "to participate" which clearly refers to cultural freedom. The first international document to include a direct reference to cultural rights in its title was the International Covenant on Economic, Social and Cultural Rights (United Nations, 1966). Article 15 of this affirms that:

1. The States Parties to the present covenant recognize the right of everyone:

    (a). To take part in cultural life;

    (b). To enjoy the benefits of scientific progress and its applications:

    (c). To benefit from the protection of the moral and material interests resulting from any scientific, literary or artistic production of which he is the author.

2. The steps to be taken by the States Parties to the present Covenant to achieve the full realization of this right shall include those necessary for the conservation, the development and the diffusion of science and culture.

3. The States Parties to the present Covenant undertake to respect the freedom indispensable for scientific research and creative activity.

4. The States Parties to the present Covenant recognize the benefits to be derived from the encouragement and development of international contacts and co-operation in the scientific and cultural fields.

Donders (2004) underlines that the concept of culture in the context of Article 15 referred exclusively to national culture, since the member countries rejected a UNESCO proposal to include the right to participate in the cultural life of the community: "The specific purpose of the right to take part in cultural life was to ensure that culture in its classic form had to be made more accessible to the masses, not just to a small elite. Culture still had limited meaning: it was mainly approached as a product including its cultural materials, such as arts and literature, not as a process. The aspects of a broader concept of culture, such as language, religion and education, were dealt with in a separate article in the human rights instruments." She also indicates that "the right to take part in cultural life at that time did not imply the right of all people to enjoy these cultural activities that they themselves found worthwhile. Cultural access did not mean that the masses could rule on which cultural activities should be available and accessible." She says that even though the wording of the article has not changed over the years, the UN Committee on Economic, Social and Cultural Rights did adopt revised guidelines for the report that the members states are required to deliver.

Article IV of the Declaration of Principles of International Cultural Co-operation (United Nations, 1966) acknowledges that one of the objectives of cultural co-operation is "to enable everyone to have access to knowledge, to enjoy the arts and literature of all peoples, to share advances made in science in all parts of the world and in the resulting benefits, and to contribute to the enrichment of cultural life". Its Article I also states that:

1. Each culture has a dignity and value which must be respected and preserved.

2. Every people has the right and the duty to develop its culture.

3. In their rich variety and diversity, and in the reciprocal influences they exert on one another, all cultures form part of the common heritage belonging to all mankind.

The UNESCO Recommendation on Participation by the People at Large in Cultural Life and Their Contribution to It (1976) deals with a broad definition of culture and recognises that access and participation have a relation to all dimensions of life. It underlines the role of active participation of peoples and implies cultural policies as well as states' obligations to recognise cultural rights as human rights. "Access may promote participation in cultural life and participation may broaden access to culture by endowing it with its true meaning."

There are other international and national documents that have great importance. These include the Charter of the United Nations and the Constitution of UNESCO. In the 1990s there were several international and national projects on ethics in cultural policies and international action plans for cultural policies. The report of the World Commission on Culture and Development, *Our creative diversity* (1995), includes recommendations to the international community related to cultural rights. The report also suggests creating an ombudsman to follow the fulfilment of cultural rights. Amongst other instruments are the UNESCO Action

Plan on Cultural Policies for Development (Stockholm Declaration, 1988), according to which promotion of cultural life can be broken down into different points including promotion of local, creative and participatory cultural life, multicultural education and fostering the role of culture in social transformation processes.

Other relevant documents include: the UNESCO Declaration of Principles of International Cultural Co-operation (1966), as well as the Declaration on Race and Racial Prejudice (UNESCO, 1978), the International Convention on the Elimination of All Forms of Racial Discrimination (UN, 1965), the Convention concerning the Protection of the World Cultural and Natural Heritage (UNESCO, 1972), the Convention on the Elimination of All Forms of Discrimination against Women (UN, 1979), the Declaration on the Right to Development (UN, 1986), the Convention on the Rights of the Child (UN, 1989), the Declaration on the Rights of Persons Belonging to National or Ethnic, Religious and Linguistic Minorities (UN, 1992), the Declaration on the Rights of Indigenous Peoples (UN, 2007), the Convention for the Safeguarding of the Intangible Cultural Heritage (UNESCO, 2006) and the Convention on the Protection and Promotion of the Diversity of Cultural Expressions (UNESCO, 2005), among others.

The Human Development Report 2004, *Cultural liberty in today's diverse world*, includes indicators on cultural freedom as a measure of human development. One of the main findings of the report is that cultural freedom is fundamental to human development as people are able to make multiple choices for their own well-being without being discriminated against because of their cultural identity. The report suggests that a way has to be found to tackle cultural exclusion through the participatory design of multicultural public policies and actions resulting from them.

At the European intergovernmental level, the Council of Europe is the most active institution as regards legislation on cultural rights. The main reference instruments are the European Convention on Human Rights (also known as the Convention for the Protection of Human Rights and Fundamental Freedoms, Council of Europe, 1950) and the European Cultural Convention (Council of Europe, 1954), both of which were drafted in the aftermath of the Universal Declaration of Human Rights and do not reflect cultural freedoms to a large extent. In the European Convention on Human Rights the articles with cultural content are the ones that include references to fundamental freedoms such as the right to freedom of thought, conscience and religion (Article 9), freedom of expression (Article 10) and freedom of assembly and association (Article 11). The European Cultural Convention underlines the importance of safeguarding the development and existence of European languages (Article 2), promotion of European cultural activities (Article 3) and European heritage (Article 5). The Charter of Fundamental Rights of the European Union from 2000 includes – together with the above-mentioned fundamental freedoms – the freedom of the arts and sciences (Article 13), the right to education (Article 14), non-discrimination (Article 21), cultural, religious and linguistic diversity (Article 22) and equality between men and women (Article 23).

The European Social Charter (1961, revised in 1996) puts in place a system in which the member states of the Council of Europe are periodically surveyed on the implementation of the social rights listed in the Charter. In the case of cultural rights, this kind of procedure does not exist except insofar as the Committee on Economic, Social and Cultural Rights of the United Nations periodically requires reports from the member states on the actions taken as regards the provisions in the International Covenant on Economic, Social and Cultural Rights, including Article 15. The Covenant recognised the right to information, and the right of persons with disabilities to participate in the life of the community, together with the right to protection against poverty and social exclusion (including access to culture).

The European Declaration on Cultural Objectives, adopted by the 4th Conference of European Ministers Responsible for Cultural Affairs (Berlin, 1984), Council of Europe, states, *inter alia*:

Promoting participation

10. To enable everyone to contribute to the shaping of ideas and to participate in choices which determine the future; and accordingly to provide everyone with maximum access to the relevant information;

11. To ensure that community action – or action taken on behalf of the community – is clearly explained, publicly debated and democratically decided upon and implemented;

12. To promote recognition of the culture of the regions, migrants and minorities and their participation in the community, so that our society – mindful of such diversity – will allow the emergence of new forms of social cohesion.

The 1984 European Declaration on Cultural Objectives of the Council of Europe designates participation in cultural life as one of the main elements for cultural policies in Europe. The promotion of participation according to the declaration includes community action and recognition of cultural diversity and the rights of minorities to participate in cultural life in order to contribute to shaping a cohesive society. Other instruments include the European Charter for Regional or Minority Languages (1992) and the Framework Convention for the Protection of National Minorities (1995).

In the 1990s both UNESCO and the Council of Europe elaborated an institutional debate on cultural rights within their structures and strategies. UNESCO published its *Medium-term strategy 1996-2001* and the Council of Europe, after the 1st Summit of Heads of State and Government in Vienna in October 1993, decided to make political commitments and draft instruments focused on the realisation of rights of cultural minorities.

The Council of Europe held a "think tank" meeting on cultural rights in January 1994 that formed the initial stage in the process of drafting a list of cultural rights that could serve to underpin an international legal instrument.[6] The conclusions of the meeting underlined the universality of cultural rights and the necessity to come up with a proper definition as well as follow-up structures for cultural rights. Participation in cultural life was listed as one of the basic cultural rights.

In 1997, the Council of Europe published the report *In from the margins: a contribution to the debate on culture and development in Europe*, which aimed at studying the condition of cultural policies in Europe and the relationship between culture and development as addressed in *Our creative diversity* (1995) a couple of years earlier. The main thesis of the report was to bring culture in from the margins to the centre of societies, at the same time promoting creative diversity as encouraged in the UNESCO report. The Council of Europe report fosters the idea that four principles – identity, participation, diversity and creativity – are fundamental in cultural policy making.

---

6. The meeting was part of the follow-up to the Council's 1st Summit and preparation for the 62nd Session of the Council for Cultural Co-operation and a response to the "Human rights and genuine democracy" group's request to elaborate a list of cultural rights together with the Committee on the European Social Charter and the Steering Committee for Human Rights.

The 1996 draft declaration of cultural rights was put together by the Fribourg Group (of the Interdisciplinary Institute of Ethics and Human Rights of the University of Fribourg, Switzerland) in collaboration with UNESCO, the Council of Europe and the Swiss National Commission for UNESCO. The work was developed along two main lines: clarification of existing cultural rights and examination of the cultural dimension of existing human rights. The draft included six main cultural rights in which cultural identity had a central role. One of the fundamental ideas is that the right to participate in cultural life is an integral part of individual freedom and social creativity.

This approach acknowledges that cultural rights guarantee the connections between the diversity of knowledge and the diversity of actors that constitute a state of a "society in learning", where rights are individual and collective at the same time – since the individuals are collective actors who take their values to the civil, cultural, economic and political space. The idea is that an individual can develop completely only if cultural rights and cultural citizenship are fully embraced. In this thinking, cultural rights are the foundation of development because they support the integration of multiple individual and social capacities. The cultural rights mentioned in the declaration include: fundamental cultural rights – the right to choose and expect respect for one's own culture; to get to know, see and respect one another's culture; to gain access to and participate in heritage; to be able to refer to a cultural community; to enjoy freedom of language, communication and creation; the right to education, training and adequate information; and the right to participate in cultural life. Patrice Meyer-Bisch from the Fribourg Group underlines the distinction between positive and negative state obligations and indicates that the third sector, for-profit organisations and states (as actors in the public space), are concerned with different rights. His recommendation for the public authorities is not only to support cultural development, but also to foster it through the promotion of interaction between cultural actors. This requires the active participation of civil society in institutional networks, the creation of independent observation networks, and pressure for political change through the monitoring, protection and valuing of the diversity of cultural heritage as a common human resource.

The working group adopted, in 2007, the Fribourg Declaration on Cultural Rights, which is a useful compilation of existing instruments. The text was presented by the Observatory of Diversity and Cultural Rights (the headquarters of which are at the Interdisciplinary Institute of Ethnics and Human Rights at Fribourg University) together with the Organisation internationale de la Francophonie and UNESCO. The

33

12 articles of the declaration cover a variety of aspects such as cultural identity, cultural communities, access and participation, education and training, communication and information, cultural co-operation, democratic governance, cultural economy, and social and global responsibility. On access and participation (Article 5) the declaration states:

Article 5 (access to and participation in cultural life)

a. Everyone, alone or in community with others, has the right to access and participate freely in cultural life through the activities of one's choice, regardless of frontiers.

b. This right includes in particular:

- The freedom to express oneself, in public or in private in the language(s) of one's choice;
- The freedom to exercise, in conformity with the rights recognised in the present Declaration, one's own cultural practices and to follow a way of life associated with the promotion of one's cultural resources, notably in the area of the use of and in the production of goods and services;
- The freedom to develop and share knowledge and cultural expressions, to conduct research and to participate in different forms of creation as well as to benefit from these;
- The right to the presentation of the moral and material interests linked to the works that result from one's cultural activity.

The Council of Europe Framework Convention on the Value of Cultural Heritage for Society, adopted at Faro on 27 October 2005, is one of the few existing instruments on equal access to and participation in heritage (explicitly mentioned in Article 5.*d* – the commitment of the member states to create conditions for participation in cultural heritage activities and in Article 12). It has yet to enter into force, as 10 ratifications are needed and only eight have been received to date. The convention acknowledges that "knowledge and use of heritage form part of the citizen's right to participate in cultural life as defined in the Universal Declaration of Human Rights". The convention shifts from the classical preservation of heritage to democratic participation, and citizens' rights and responsibilities, in order to protect the common memory and heritage in the context of globalisation. The convention has its roots in the Council's work on identity, heritage and diversity and is a result of new thinking that recognises that heritage is a common good, the protection of which should be a shared responsibility of communities and which forms a fundamental element of cultural life of Europe.

The convention states, *inter alia*:

Article 12 – Access to cultural heritage and democratic participation

The Parties undertake to:

a. encourage everyone to participate in:
  - the process of identification, study, interpretation, protection, conservation and presentation of the cultural heritage;
  - public reflection and debate on the opportunities and challenges which the cultural heritage represents;

b. take into consideration the value attached by each heritage community to the cultural heritage with which it identifies;

c. recognise the role of voluntary organisations both as partners in activities and as constructive critics of cultural heritage policies;

d. take steps to improve access to the heritage, especially among young people and the disadvantaged, in order to raise awareness about its value, the need to maintain and preserve it, and the benefits which may be derived from it.

One of the main problems in the follow-up to enjoyment of cultural rights is the lack of monitoring systems. Countries do present reports to the United Nations Committee on Economic, Social and Cultural Rights on the fulfilment of different rights mentioned in the covenant, but there is no legal obligation to do so nor is the content of the right to participate in cultural life defined exhaustively.

2.4 Local and regional environment

This study concentrates on public policies and states' plans of action, but mention should be made of the local and regional environment because it is at the local level that so many of the contentious issues related to co-existence are most visible. Far from the frameworks of international guidelines and national policy principles, local policies are often forced to respond rapidly to different challenges. While local cultural policies often need to tackle emerging problems quickly, national policies take longer to be devised and implemented. Whereas locally the environment needs to cater for physical access and opportunities for interaction, the participation element in national policies is often about legal and political recognition.

The change in the traditional role of states has brought about a change in the balance of power relationships. That has in turn activated the contribution of local and regional authorities in building an enabling environment for the enjoyment of participation and cultural rights. In many European countries, the "subjects" of cultural policies are increasingly involved in the design and execution of policies, including cultural policies, thanks to the growing importance of local and regional authorities. This involves a transfer of responsibilities and an increase of local elements in the design of policies. Decentralisation is the basis for democratisation of decision-making processes in which local processes begin to acquire an important role.

Inevitably, the local level is the space where cultural conflicts in everyday life are played out. International legal instruments may have a guiding role in local settings, but the real issue is how to turn them into successful policies. At the local level, culture can function as a fundamental exercise of citizenship, autonomy and liberty. Equally, but sadly, it can be the source of social fragmentation and lack of communication between members of the community. Cultural policies at the local level need to have strong ethical dimensions. They play a crucial role in strengthening social cohesion, participation, democracy and equality, and in building a sense of belonging to a community.

Local processes that aim at fostering participation in cultural life have a long history. The community arts movement was launched in marginalised communities in North America and in Europe in the 1970s with the idea that active participation in cultural life is essential for the cultural development of a community and for strengthening the role of culture as a social transformer.

Some reports show that cultural management depends essentially on the communities' actions and the local political will. The communities and cities have different knowledge and financial bases to foster cultural emancipation and to help the participation of all social groups. One example, of many such reports, is the study carried out by the Working Group on Young People and Culture of EUROCITIES[7] on access of young people to culture, which presents a set of best practices in European cities that highlight the connection between arts, culture, education and the labour market. Another example is the cultural strategy paper of Leicester (2001) on *Access to culture – The cultural needs and rights of individuals* that has as an objective "to invest in the development of cultural activity that contributes to the economic, social and personal well-being of individuals at all stages of their lives and to increase access to, and participation in, cultural activity". The strategy includes a public consultation (4 May 2001) and 11 key challenges for creating equal access to culture, freedom of cultural expression for everyone and the opportunity for all to fulfil their own potential. In addition, the cultural strategy outlines 80 challenges under seven key objectives for the city, which vary from small, local projects to large-scale culture-led regeneration in Leicester. The strategy paper states that "The Cultural Strategy is underpinned by the Cultural Strategy Action Plan. The first Action Plan was completed and reported on in 2004 with 61 out of 62 projects successfully implemented. The Action Plan has been developed alongside the Strategy, to monitor cultural projects and activities working to achieve this aim which are undertaken by CSP Partners."

It focuses specifically on the ways in which culture and cultural services can change our city. Our definition of culture is about improving the quality of life and well-being of Leicester's residents, workers and visitors through the provision and development of cultural activities, events and facilities and by helping to achieve other quality of life goals such as providing lifelong learning opportunities, improving health, stimulating economic development and helping to improve safety and cohesion in our communities.

Cultural activity is linked with people's identity, confidence, self-esteem, joy and pleasure. It helps people learn. It helps them stay healthy. It helps communities grow together, understand each other and discover shared experience. It helps neighbourhoods and the city as a whole to develop a sense of place, and culture brings jobs and wealth to the city. The vitality that comes from having many different

7. A European network with more than 130 city members in over 30 countries.

cultures living and working together is expressed everyday in Leicester through a range of cultural activity – such as arts, sports, libraries, museums, heritage, archives, architecture, children's play, parks, tourism, creative industries, media and markets.

Leicester Cultural Strategy. Leicester City Council, 2001

In a paper commissioned by the Institute of Culture of Barcelona City Council and the Working Group on Culture of the United Cities and Local Governments the team led by Nancy Duxbury stated that "culturally vibrant cities are ensuring citizens who participate in diverse cultural activities as leaders and as volunteers are recognised and appreciated, thereby encouraging more citizen involvement at a grass-roots level".

In recent years, Agenda 21 for Culture is one of the most successful models for integrating participatory principles into urban policy planning. Jordi Pascual i Ruiz calls it "a declaration of cities for cultural rights". Agenda 21 for Culture, with its 67 articles (combining principles, undertakings and recommendations), was approved by cities and local governments in May 2004, resulting later in its adoption as a reference document by United Cities and Local Governments. Agenda 21 for Culture has a very strong participatory and rights-based approach to policy planning and programming at local, regional, national, international and organisational level. It adopted a set of recommendations for reinforcing democratic cultural policies at the local level including "the encouragement and stimulation of the democratic participation of citizens in the formulation, exercise and evaluation of public policies on culture". Furthermore, the document on the implementation of Agenda 21 for Culture offers four possible tools that could prove useful in general policy planning as well. These tools include a local cultural strategy that takes into account the local cultural priorities; the drafting of a local charter on cultural rights and responsibilities that reflects the needs and perceptions of the local population; the establishment of a culture council that deals with a variety of cultural issues in the city; and carrying out cultural impact assessments to measure the impact of different actions on local cultural life.

3. Participation in culture in the administration and legislation

Former UNESCO Director General René Maheu acknowledged that the right to take part in and access cultural life is a fundamental feature in modern states. Cultural policies are about assuring the quality of life and enjoyment of the citizen. Members of any society should feel that they are included, properly represented and respected – and that the policies, decisions and practices of government, administrations and society reflect this. To provide access for everyone to cultural life, and to create an enabling environment for participation tends to contribute to long-term social cohesion.

This chapter provides an overview of the main concepts (cultural rights, access, participation, cultural provision, etc.) in the administration and legislation of European countries and a general synopsis of existing policies (principles and plans of action), legislative processes and the current debate on participatory cultural policies. It is not intended to be an exhaustive review but to offer an overview of elements.

There are several publications on cultural policies in Europe that include a discussion of access, provision and participation in cultural life. The 1997 Council of Europe publication *In from the margins: a contribution to the debate on culture and development in Europe* offers an overview of the values in European cultural policy making, based on ideas from the 1970s and earlier that fostered the strengthening of national identity, cultural diversity and creativity. It advocated the provision of cultural services, especially for those living in less privileged conditions.

3.1 Assuring access – The legal approach

In order to foster cultural well-being in its citizens, a state needs to adopt policies that ensure that every citizen encounters an enabling environment for cultural experience. Such policies need a legal base that guarantees cultural rights so that they are not a gift of political will, but a fundamental part of a citizen's entitlement. One of the main tasks of an administration is to have a solid legal or regulatory system that enables people to access and take part in the cultural activities of their own choice. The acknowledgement of these rights imposes an obligation on the state or other administration to promote, provide and fulfil them. There is also an implicit requirement on the citizen to observe the basic principles of respect and non-discrimination as regards the rights of others. General international instruments have direct and indirect effects on the domestic legal framework for policy. However, there are no substantial analyses available of the contents of the right to access or participation.

In the literature the emphasis is often placed on the development of international instruments rather than domestic ones. Kim (2006) quotes Häberle who affirms that legal provisions should be made for tradition, innovation and pluralism as the three pillars of culture. Kim adds spirituality, autonomy, and openness as features for protection and promotion by a state in order to encourage an open culture for and by everybody.

In Europe, the legal instruments that refer to access to and participation in culture are mainly found in constitutional frameworks. In constitutional law, the references to cultural rights, access to and participation in cultural life do not come together. The great majority of countries refer to human rights as a basis for equal treatment and non-discrimination, as well as to fundamental freedoms (the freedom of expression, religion, assembly, association, opinion, etc.) and the right to life. These can be interpreted as requirements for a dignified and fulfilled life, of which cultural activity forms a part. All freedoms have a culturally participatory aspect to them, such as the freedom of speech or opinion – in which case the citizen should have access to the means to express himself/herself. The right to education is also present in several framework instruments, even though for the most part it is not considered a participatory right as such. Nevertheless, while the development of legal rights is a sign of concern from a state or other public administration, if it is not accompanied by effective policy planning, design and attitudes the effect does not reach much beyond declarations and texts.

Most of the countries with constitutions dating back to the beginning of the 20th century have included human rights in later amendments, with the exception of Austria. In those rare cases where cultural rights and participation in cultural life are mentioned, they refer mostly to minority rights and to the rights of cultural producers and creators rather than to the rights of the general public to cultural experiences. In the case of Germany, even if there is only one reference to culture in the constitution, most of the constitutions of the *Länder* contain numerous references to cultural issues, including aspects of access and participation.

When it comes to legal elements that refer to access to and participation in cultural life, cultural democracy or the right to enjoy culture in its various forms, countries have different approaches. "Cultural democracy" is rarely mentioned in constitutions themselves. An exception is the Portuguese Constitution of 1976. In Article 2, on the democratic state and rule of law – the fundamental principles of the constitution – it makes a reference to participatory processes in order to achieve a state of economic, social and cultural democracy.

The Portuguese Constitution also includes a large spectrum of different rights related to culture which is exceptional in the European, and global, setting.

> The Portuguese Constitution refers to many aspects of cultural participation and makes a direct reference to cultural rights (as the task of the state to realise the economic, social and cultural rights of the citizen, in Article 9.*d*), the freedom of cultural creation (Article 42), the cultural rights of young people (Article 70), the rights of people with disabilities (Article 71), the cultural rights of elderly people (Article 72), as well as the right to culture. The latter is mentioned in Chapter III on cultural rights and duties; including the right to culture, democratisation of culture and access to culture and creation (Article 73), the right to cultural enjoyment and creation – including access to the means and instruments of cultural action (Article 78). The Portuguese Constitution requires the state to play an active role and lists as some of its tasks the need to secure cultural conditions, participatory democracy and cultural rights of citizens.

Article 73 of the Portuguese Constitution (1976) on education, culture and science states:

1. Everyone has the right to education and culture.

2. The State promotes the democratisation of education and other conditions so that education at school and by other methods can contribute to the development of the personality, to social progress, and to democratic participation in public life.

3. In conjunction with the mass media, cultural association and trusts, cultural and recreational groups, associations for the safeguard of the cultural heritage, neighbourhood organizations and other cultural agents, the State promotes the democratization of culture by encouraging and securing access by all citizens to the fruits of culture and cultural creation.

4. Scientific creation and research, as well as technological innovation, is encouraged and assisted by the State.

Other European constitutions are less comprehensive in terms of cultural participatory rights. However, there are other examples where they are touched upon. Some constitutions recognise the rights to participation in cultural life, cultural identity, own culture and language and other relevant aspects related to cultural participation. Some countries identify specific target groups for these rights whilst others describe the rights in more general terms.

Participation in cultural life is mentioned in the Georgian Constitution (Article 34) together with the development of culture, expression and enrichment of cultural origins, and recognition of national and generic values and international cultural relations. The constitution also recognises the equality of citizens in Georgia in different dimensions of public life, including cultural life, together with the rights of the free use of language and development of culture (Article 38). Georgia also has a Law on Culture (1977) to secure citizens' cultural rights and the maintenance of cultural values. The law gives the individual the right to carry out cultural and creative activities as regards his or her own interests and abilities.

The Hungarian Constitution is another case. Article 66 ensures equality between men and women regarding all civil, political, economic, social and cultural rights. A similar article can be found in the Maltese Constitution (Article 14 on gender equality). Furthermore, the Hungarian Constitution designates the government as the body responsible for determining the role of the state in cultural and scientific development (Article 35). The Hungarian Constitution also recognises the rights of national and ethnic minorities and ensures their collective participation in public life as well as related cultural rights (Article 68). It also ensures freedom of artistic expression (Article 70G) and the right of its citizens to education/culture (70F – the wording of the latter is sometimes mistakenly interpreted as solely the right to education but the Hungarian language offers the possibility of understanding this part as a larger aspect that includes culture).

Azerbaijan's Law on Culture acknowledges the right to cultural identity, whilst other legislation supports this provision as well. In addition, the 1998 Culture Act ensures the right to engage in creative activity. The right to one's own culture and language is also recognised in the Finnish Constitution (Article 17). This article also refers to the rights of the Sami people to develop and maintain their culture.

The Constitution of Moldova guarantees the participation of young people in culture (Article 50) as well as the right to the preservation of cultural identity (Article 10), and freedom to create (Article 33). The Croatian Constitution (from 1990, latest amendment in 2001) contains several references to cultural rights. In the preamble, the promotion of cultural progress is mentioned together with human rights and freedoms as well as social progress. In the articles themselves, mention is made of the expression of cultural convictions through associations (Article 43), protection of youth and providing a decent life through adequate conditions such as culture (Article 62), freedom of artistic creativity and promotion of cultural development (Article 68) – this article also contains a reference to the protection of national cultural values. Minorities also have a right to cultural autonomy with respective rights (Article 15).

The right to participate in cultural life is mentioned in the Armenian Constitution (Article 36), the Spanish Constitution (Article 9), as well as in the Russian Constitution (Article 44.2). The latter's Article 44 recognises the right to use institutions of culture and to access cultural values. The 1992 Basic Law on Culture of the Russian Federation guarantees cultural rights and liberties in the cultural field. An update of this law has been planned but so far it has yet to materialise.

Keeping in mind the progressive importance given to culture in legal environments, it is quite understandable that recent constitutions or constitutions with recent amendments have more references to cultural rights, if not in terms of the general public then with regard to the access to culture of specific groups.

The Constitution of "the former Yugoslav Republic of Macedonia" (1991) mentions cultural rights in various articles – freedom and protection of economic, social and cultural rights in Article 20; ethnic, cultural and spiritual rights in Article 48; and the cultural rights of Macedonian citizens living abroad in Article 49. It also acknowledges the freedom of creation and the protection of the development of arts and culture (Article 47).

The revision of the Romanian Constitution, adopted by a constitutional referendum in 2003, includes, for example, the right of national minorities to use their native language in public administration. Its Article 7 also refers to Romanians living abroad and the opportunity to strengthen their cultural identity when living outside Romania, acknowledging the possibility for Romanians to participate in the cultural life even if physically in another country. Article 33 of the Romanian Constitution recognises the right to access culture:

Article 33 – Access to culture

1. The access to culture is guaranteed under the law.

2. A person's freedom to develop his/her spirituality and to get access to the values of national and universal culture shall not be limited.

3. The State must make sure that spiritual identity is preserved, national culture is supported, arts are stimulated, cultural legacy is protected and preserved, contemporary creativity is developed and Romania's cultural and artistic values are promoted throughout the world.

The 1997 Polish Constitution underlines equal access to cultural goods, and also action to facilitate access to Polish culture for Polish people living abroad (Article 6). Article 35 guarantees the cultural rights and freedoms of people belonging to minorities, and Article 73 refers to artistic freedom and use of cultural assets. Poland also has a Law on Museums (1996) that stipulates free admission to public museums one day per week and reduced ticket prices.

Even if a direct reference to the right to participate in cultural life might be absent in some constitutions, the cultural rights of minorities fill the gap in some. For example, the 1922 Latvian Constitution recognises the right of cultural minorities to preserve and develop their cultural identity. The Serbian Constitution has several articles that mention self-governance, non-discrimination and the partial cultural autonomy of minorities. It also acknowledges the participation in cultural life of minorities (Article 76) and it recognises the concept of cultural diversity and its promotion (Article 48). In the Slovakian Constitution, the cultural rights of minorities are listed in Article 34 of the constitution.

The Lithuanian Constitution (1992) recognises in Article 37 the right of people belonging to ethnic communities to foster their language, culture and customs. Article 42 recognises the extent of culture and the support the state should give to culture and science. Article 44 prohibits censorship and mass media monopolisation, and Article 45 gives autonomy to ethnic communities to administer the affairs of their ethnic culture, education and organisations. This article once again recognises the state's role in the support of ethnic communities.

The Ukrainian Constitution (1996, amended in 2004) recognises in Article 11 the consolidation and development of the Ukrainian nation, including its culture, and in the same article the state's duty to promote the development of the ethnic, linguistic and religious identity of all indigenous peoples and national minorities. As in the Romanian Constitution, the Ukrainian one also recognises that the state is required to provide nationals residing abroad with access to their national, cultural and linguistic needs. Article 24 refers to the equality of men and women in different spheres of social life, including cultural activity.

Even if not referring to cultural rights or specific groups, some European constitutions refer to cultural development, the protection and promotion of culture, or to cultural welfare.

Article 8 of the Maltese Constitution notes the state's duty to promote the development of culture and the Swedish Constitution makes a reference to cultural welfare. The Dutch Constitution has only one reference to culture – that is, the promotion of social and cultural development and leisure activities listed under Article 22 on health. The article was included in the 1983 complete revision of the constitution, and Article 22 mentioned rights that were too important to be left out, yet considered not important enough to have a separate article (health, housing, culture and recreation).

The Italian Constitution acknowledges the promotion of cultural development (Article 9) and the freedom of the arts (Article 33). Article 117 recognises the decentralisation of certain responsibilities including cultural administration, giving the responsibility of "the promotion and organisation of cultural activities" to the regions. However, legislation regarding the division of responsibilities is unclear, reflecting several changes in the legislative framework.

Access to cultural life can also be understood as a more extensive term than solely providing the means of access.

In Belgium, it seems that the right to culture is understood as a large concept that is not limited to access, but includes taking an active role. In Article 23 of the Belgian Constitution there is a reference to the right to lead a life in conformity with human dignity and cultural rights (amongst other human rights). Related to this is the right to enjoy cultural and social fulfilment.[8] The Flemish Community also has a decree concerning sociocultural work (4/4/2003).

45

8. See: www.senate.be/doc/const_fr.html.

The right to access to culture for everyone, and of young people to cultural development, is also mentioned in the Spanish Constitution (Articles 44 and 48). It recognises the linguistic and cultural pluralism of the country in its preamble. Linguistic and cultural pluralism is mentioned in the Belgian and Cypriot constitutions. The Slovakian Constitution notes the right of access to heritage by the public.

The right to education and access, and the right to information, are frequent features in constitutional law but only a few countries mention artistic education in their constitutional frameworks. However, there are a couple of examples.

Article 38 of the Estonian Constitution requires that science and arts education must exist freely. The Romanian Constitution refers to the freedom of religious education in its Article 32. The Greek Constitution lists the freedom of the arts together with the freedom of education and research.

As regards other aspects, some countries recognise the importance of creativity and arts, or cultural expression.

The Bulgarian Constitution (from 1991, last amendment in 2006) has an article on culture and creativity. Article 53.1 recognises that "everyone shall have the right to avail himself of the national and universal human cultural values and to develop his own culture in accordance with his ethnic self-identification, which shall be recognised and guaranteed by the law". The Slovenian Constitution (1991) acknowledges the right to cultural expression (Article 61), linguistic rights (Article 62) and rights of minorities (Articles 64 and 65); Article 71 protects the cultural advancement and the land of the people living in mountainous areas.

Citizens' cultural duties are hardly mentioned in the various constitutions. There are, however, some exceptions to be found.

The Romanian Constitution acknowledges the sacred faithfulness that the citizen should hold towards the country and the conditions of good faith that should prevail when rights and freedoms are exercised. The Georgian Constitution states that every citizen of Georgia is obliged to protect and preserve the cultural heritage (Article 34). The Constitution of Azerbaijan recognises citizens' duty to protect historical and cultural monuments (Article 77) and, as a counterpart to the right to culture, respect the historical, cultural and spiritual inheritance (Article 40). The Slovakian Constitution lists the duty to protect cultural heritage (Article 44), which is also mentioned in the 2006 Serbian Constitution (Article 89) and in the Russian Constitution (Article 44.3). The Swiss Constitution mentions the "assistance to cultural integration of children" (Article 41).

The Portuguese Constitution lists the cultural duties of heritage preservation as a result of access to creation and leisure:

Article 78 – Cultural enjoyment and creation

1. Everyone has the right to cultural enjoyment and creation, and the duty to preserve, defend, and increase the cultural heritage.

The Constitution of Azerbaijan connects the right to take part in cultural life with the duty to respect cultural heritage:

Article 40 – Right to culture

1. Everyone has the right to take part in cultural life, to use organisations and values of culture.

2. Everyone must respect historical, cultural and spiritual inheritance, take care of it, and protect historical and cultural memorials.

As stated before, early 20th-century constitutions have fewer references to cultural rights and fewer still to participation in cultural life.

The case of the Norwegian Constitution is an interesting one, as it is one of the few, if not the only, constitution in the world written in a foreign language. The Norwegian Constitution – the oldest constitution still in force in Europe – is dated 1814 when Danish was still the official written language. Even though the constitution underwent some linguistic changes in 1903, it remained close to the original. However, for example, in the case of the rights of the Sami people (Article 110.a of the constitution),[9] the word "Sami" (*samisk*) was not common until the 1970s. In 1903 it would have been more common to use the word "Lappish" (*lappisk*) but this is considered to be a derogatory term in today's Norway.

The 1935 Irish Constitution has no reference to cultural rights, only to the right of the state to develop the national culture. However, other legislative instruments serve to complement the constitution. One of the

---

9. Article 110.a: "It is the responsibility of the authorities of the State to create conditions enabling the Sami people to preserve and develop its language, culture and way of life", *Kongeriket Norge* (the Norwegian Constitution).

main cultural policy objectives in Ireland is to develop cultural and arts legislation. The legislative framework is basically covered in the Arts Act (2003) and partly in the Local Government Act (1994), which gives local administrations the possibility to formulate cultural and arts policy, but neither of the acts includes references to cultural rights or participation.

Even if some countries do not have references to culture in their constitutional framework, the legislation in force does offer certain solutions. The United Kingdom has no written constitution. Constitutional law there is an amalgam of tradition, precedent and treaties. Consequently, cultural rights are assumed (though untested in the courts) to stem from common law rights, the 1689 English Bill of Rights and the Scottish Claim of Right, and the recent integration of the European conventions. In France *la loi d'orientation* against exclusion mentions in Chapter 5 that: "the equal access to everyone throughout their lives to culture, sport, vacation time and leisure constitutes a national objective. This guarantees an effective exercise of citizenship. The realisation of this objective implies the development of priority forms of less favoured areas, artistic, cultural and sport activities." The Russian Federation has a Law on National Cultural Autonomy that provides the legal basis for cultural self-organisation in the diaspora areas (in 2006 there were 621 culturally autonomous areas).

As for recent international instruments, as of September 2009, 34 European countries had approved, ratified or otherwise recognised the UNESCO Convention on the Protection and Promotion of the Diversity of Cultural Expressions. Croatia (12 May 2006) and Romania (20 July 2006) were the first European countries to ratify the convention, followed by several other European countries at the end of 2006.

Legal elements related to access and participation in cultural life in European constitutional frameworks

Elements related to access to and participation in cultural life	Cultural participation rights and rights related to access to culture in the constitutional frameworks of European countries
Access to culture and/or cultural creation	Hungary (of young people), France (of young people), Portugal, Romania, Spain
Access to cultural conditions for all	Portugal
Access to heritage	Slovakia
Access to means and instruments of cultural action	Portugal
Access to the products of culture	Poland
Access to values of national and universal culture	Bulgaria, Romania
Assistance to cultural integration of children	Switzerland
Assuring cultural conditions for all	Portugal
Cultural associations, cultural groups, neighbourhood associations	Croatia, Hungary, Poland, Portugal
Cultural conditions in health	Georgia (healthy environment and cultural surroundings), Portugal (of young people, the disabled and elderly)
Cultural co-operation	Georgia
Cultural democracy	Portugal
(References to) cultural rights	Belgium (as part of human dignity), Hungary, "the former Yugoslav Republic of Macedonia", Malta (gender equality), Portugal
Cultural rights of minorities	Albania, Armenia, Azerbaijan, Belgium, Bulgaria, Croatia (explicit mention of minority cultural rights), Georgia, Estonia (specific law on cultural and ethnic minorities), Finland, Hungary, Latvia, Lithuania, Montenegro, Norway, Romania, Russian Federation, Serbia, Slovakia (explicit mention of minority cultural rights), Slovenia, Sweden, "the former Yugoslav Republic of Macedonia", Ukraine
Cultural rights of nationals living abroad	Bulgaria
Cultural rights of specific groups	Croatia (adequate cultural conditions of life for young people), Hungary (young people), France (young people), Portugal (young people, the disabled and elderly), Romania (participation in cultural life of young people)

49

Elements related to access to and participation in cultural life	Cultural participation rights and rights related to access to culture in the constitutional frameworks of European countries
Cultural values	Bulgaria (with reference to universal cultural values), Croatia (with reference to cultural goods), Georgia, Montenegro, the Russian Federation
Dignified cultural life	Belgium
Equality in cultural life	Georgia
Freedom of creativity, creation or artistic expression	Albania, Armenia, Azerbaijan, Belgium, Bulgaria, Croatia, Estonia, Hungary, Latvia, Macedonia, Moldova, Poland, Portugal, Russian Federation, Slovakia, Slovenia, Spain, Turkey, Ukraine. In the case of Georgia the wording is "freedom of intellectual creativity", in the case of Bulgaria it is "recognition of artistic creativity" and in the case of Lithuania "unrestrictiveness of culture"
Freedom of expression, information, press and religion	Most countries
Promotion or protection of cultural development, progress, arts or arts education	Bulgaria (including state support for talented students), Croatia (cultural progress and development of culture), Georgia, Germany, Greece, Hungary, Malta. In Belgium, the wording is "freedom of the development of the arts"
Protection of arts and artists	Turkey
Protection of cultural heritage	Portugal
Preservation of cultural identity	Bulgaria, Moldova, Montenegro
Provision of cultural welfare	Sweden
Right to culture (general public)	Azerbaijan, Finland, Greece, Hungary, Latvia, Lithuania, Portugal, Sweden
Right to free development of everyone's personality	Germany, Greece
Right to participate in cultural life	Armenia, Azerbaijan, Georgia, Moldova, Portugal, Russian Federation, Spain (of young people)
Right to/promotion of cultural development/to develop or exercise culture and traditions	Azerbaijan, Belgium, Bulgaria, Georgia, Greece, Italy, "the former Yugoslav Republic of Macedonia", Malta, Netherlands, Spain. In Belgium, the wording is "freedom of the development of the arts"
Right to cultural enjoyment and creation	Portugal
Right to enjoy cultural products or goods	Poland

Elements related to access to and participation in cultural life	Cultural participation rights and rights related to access to culture in the constitutional frameworks of European countries
Protection/assistance or promotion of the development of culture	Azerbaijan, Greece, "the former Yugoslav Republic of Macedonia", Malta. In Belgium, the wording is "freedom of the development of the arts"
Quality of life	Portugal
Right to education	All (Austria and France do not mention it explicitly in their constitutions)
Citizens' obligation regarding the protection of heritage	Azerbaijan (obligation to respect cultural heritage), Georgia (protection of cultural heritage and protection of cultural surroundings), Russian Federation (obligation to preserve cultural heritage and safeguard cultural landmarks), Slovakia (obligation to protect and enhance cultural heritage)
Examples of specific legislation	Austria: freedom of the arts (Law on Civil Rights, paragraph 17.a, 1982); Azerbaijan: Law on Culture; Bulgaria: Draft Law on Youth Development including culture and cultural activities (2008); France: legislation on equal opportunities that include access to culture as a guarantee for effective citizenship (29/7/98); Georgia: Law on Culture (1977) to secure citizens' cultural rights and maintenance of cultural values; Hungary: Act LXXVII on national and ethnic minorities and the right to nurture their own language and culture (1993); Ireland: Arts Act (2003) on the responsibility of state actors to promote the development of and participation in the arts; Romania: Youth Law 350, Article 4, on the objectives of the youth policy to promote and support young people to participate in the cultural life of the country (2006); Spain: Draft Bill on Reading that underlines intellectual liberty and access to information, non-discrimination and plurality as forms of fostering reading and participation in cultural life (2006)

3.2 From laws to action –
Fostering participation in cultural life
in public administration

The policy of accessibility of culture has gone through several phases:
I Making culture (ideologically suitable) accessible to all (agit-prop cultural model of socialist countries)
II Making culture (elite culture) accessible to everyone (Malraux) – decentralisation
III Making culture (mostly elite but also amateur) accessible to different groups (i.e. groups with special needs)
IV Making cultural field accessible to all diversities of cultural expressions
V New "access society in a virtual world; two distinct civilizations – those living outside the electronic gates of cyberspace and those living on the inside" (Riffkin, 2000)

Dragićević Šešić 2009

Cultural policies in Europe are designed to serve certain democratic objectives and reflect the values of accessibility, citizens' education, freedom of creation and equal access of all to cultural goods, services and institutions. Access to and participation in cultural life are fundamental policy issues in democratic settings and in public administration the authorities are faced with the challenge of designing policies that take into account citizens and their needs. Legal instruments as frameworks for action are important, although they are neither policies nor immediate solutions.

At the policy level the real test begins with how to ensure participation and access to cultural life. Legal provision is a necessary step towards securing the enjoyment of this as of right, but the challenge comes from the translation of laws into action – from legal instruments to concrete initiatives. It is not surprising that the citizens' response to legal processes is sometimes negative as it is difficult to see their immediate application in everyday life. It is obvious that much more is needed than declarations and conventions in order to to have a real impact.

In most European countries, the administration of cultural participation policies is either the responsibility of the ministry of culture or the ministry of education. Apart from cultural policies, some ministries are also responsible for other areas – for example, church relations or religious affairs, media, sport and youth, or even some social issues. This variety complicates the comparison of the work carried out by different ministries within Europe. The framework policies related to participation in cultural life are mostly reflected in the form of state support to different activities that foster participation. These could be allocations to the cultural activities of minorities or other groups with special needs, cultural institutions or other types of funding opportunities. Other popular forms of fostering participation are policies related to libraries and education.

In some countries, decentralisation of cultural administration and federal state administration has also given decision-making powers to regional governments.

> This is the case in Austria (through the 1998 Federal Arts Promotion Act, which established the relationship between central government and the provinces in cultural matters) as well as in Germany, where cultural administration is heavily decentralised. This is also the case of Switzerland, where in general both cultural legislation and administration are heavily decentralised. In Article 69 of the constitution, the cantons are named as the authorities responsible for matters of culture. The cantons and cities have different legal approaches to fulfilling their responsibilities towards local cultural life. An example is the law of the Canton of Aargay, which decrees that 1% of the tax revenues of the previous year must be used for cultural goals.

53

In many western European countries there was already a considerable tradition of cultural democracy or democratisation of culture when cultural policy objectives came to be drafted. The idea of cultural democracy was taken up in Europe in the late 1960s and the early 1970s. Everyone should have access to and play a part in creating culture. In France, the objective of facilitating the greatest possible access to art and culture had already formed part of the mission of the ministry of culture and communication since 1959. With the then minister of culture, André Malraux, the objective of cultural democratisation was achieved with the founding of "culture houses" (*maisons de la culture*), situated in regional capitals with the support of cultural committees, which aimed at offering everyone direct access to arts and culture. This policy was based on three basic assumptions: the correction of inequality, trust in the universality and intrinsic validity of culture, and faith in the cultural democratisation process. From the 1960s onwards in France, there came a stream of new initiatives to enlarge the idea of cultural democratisation – the development of cultural infrastructure, decentralisation, an enlargement of the concept of culture, cultural mediation – culminating during the administration of culture minister Jack Lang in the 1980s. Nowadays, the French Ministry of Culture has a general programme for access to culture – *Transmission des savoirs et democratisation de la culture.*

A similar situation existed in Denmark, where the cultural policy principles started to reflect the idea of the democratisation of culture after a period during which the emphasis had been more on the dissemination of professional art. From the 1970s, the policies were intended to reflect cultural diversity and the right to pluralism as founded in the idea of cultural democracy, where cultural policy decisions were required to reflect the real needs of the people and ensure the right to creativity and self-expression. In the 1980s and 1990s, the social dimension of cultural policies was given a mainstream role: inspiring citizens' education, cultural economy and the adaptation to the new era of globalisation, new technologies and migration. The official policy of the government affirms that, "the government wishes to see a society where diversity and personal freedom flourish together with the fundamental values of the community. There should be space for diversity and for cultural and religious activity. What must be respected is the right of the individual to choose his/her own life."[10]

In the 1960s and 1970s in western European countries, cultural policy was included in the concept of the welfare state. For example, in Dutch cultural policies, cultural participation as well as the role of culture in the well-being of society became policy issues. In Austria, in the 1970s, the idea of cultural policy expanded to comprise a variety of issues to the point where it was also understood as a version of social policy. This "cultural policy turning-point" in Austria also meant the "first active dialogue between government, artists and providers of culture" with the central question being the democratisation of cultural support in decision making. In Germany, the "new cultural policy" had making the arts accessible to everyone as an objective, through the "civil right to culture" and "culture for everyone" – which led to a democratisation of culture, and the expansion of the field to include new forms that responded to demands from the public for fresh kinds of cultural services. Magdowski (2006) states: "at the latest in the 1970s there was much discussion of the question, whether the state should be using taxpayers' money to pay for art, if only a small stratum of the educated middle class (*Bildungsbürgertum*) was taking advantage of what was on offer. The demand for culture for all was born and with it the so-called democratisation of culture". As a result, today German

---

10. Danish Government policy paper (2003).

cultural policy is heavily directed toward making culture accessible to everyone. During recent years, there has been an important cultural policy debate on the link between cultural participation, citizenship and social cohesion as a result of the growing necessity for intercultural dialogue and other sociocultural issues. Although this debate has yet to be conclusive, it is considered to be of major importance.

Towards the end of the 20th century, in western European countries democratisation and decentralisation of cultural policies were complemented with the idea of social inclusion through cultural activities. The cultural offer was to reach the largest possible number of people. Acknowledgement of cultural diversity and the needs of specific groups started to gain recognition in cultural policy planning together with the operational practices of cultural institutions.

In the United Kingdom, towards the end of the last century, the themes of access and participation as well as the social impact of culture in society started to gain further importance. The United Kingdom is at the forefront of participatory cultural/arts planning, with the objective of making "the best things available to the largest possible number of people" (from the compendium report on the United Kingdom). This means special attention is paid not only to children, young people and communities, but also to ethnic minorities. Many consultation exercises with local populations have been carried out in different parts of the British Isles, the Scottish example being a very illustrative one (which is examined in greater detail later). The Department for Culture, Media and Sport in England promotes access and social inclusion, and runs programmes such as Action Team in order to bring arts and cultural activities to less-favoured neighbourhoods.

In Belgium, the right to culture is understood as action to "offer to every person the guarantee of the possibility to completely develop himself/herself through his/her view of life, ideas, thoughts, freedom of opinion and expressions of his/her aspirations".[11] However, both mobility and physical access to cultural buildings do not form part of the political competence of the federal government, but of the regions. The different communities in Belgium have slightly different cultural policy objectives. The Flemish government has implemented strategies in order to increase cultural participation and to enable people to develop their cultural capacity. The Flemish cultural policy is based on equal rights, cultural democracy and participation, and quality and diversity of the cultural opportunities on offer. According to the government policy memorandum 2004-09, the

11. "Rapport général sur la pauvreté". Available at www.mouvement-lst.org/documents/1995_rapport_general_pauvrete.pdf. Accessed in September 2009.

objective is to suppress obstacles to cultural participation through sociocultural projects, communication initiatives, awareness-raising in art and heritage institutions, and research on cultural participation. The ministry also requires that the organisations and institutions working in the field of art and culture reflect the relationship between cultural provision and the attending public. In 2001, the ministry of culture created a communication centre, CultuurNet Vlaanderen,[12] with the intention to enlarge and strengthen cultural participation and to reduce the distance between the public and the cultural activities on offer.

In the Belgian French community, one of the principal targets of cultural policies is the fostering of cultural democracy through the introduction of a variety of cultural forms to different audiences. In the programmes of the regional government and cultural organisations one of the requirements is accessibility to the public at large, especially people with socio-economic difficulties, the young and elderly people. In the Maltese framework, the aim of "democratisation culture and the arts" has been an objective since 2000 and some outreach programmes have been realised. The policy includes, for example, the interactive animation of museums in order to facilitate access to heritage. It is expected that the Maltese Council for Culture and the Arts will run programmes for democratic access and public participation, including for disabled people and refugee communities.

In central and eastern European countries, political history has meant that development has had a different focus. The transition countries have faced several challenges ranging from the restoration of national culture to structural changes in cultural administration through transformation and internationalisation. This development has followed a different rhythm in different countries and as states such as the Czech Republic, Poland and Slovenia have come towards the end of their transition, this is also reflected in the formulation of cultural policies.

Many transition countries foster both equal access and democratic participation in cultural life among their cultural policy principles.

In Croatia, policy priorities from 2004 include the promotion of cultural life and creativity with the aim that the public at large should have access to and the possibility to participate in cultural programmes and activities. Infrastructural support for participation in cultural life in conditions of equality forms part of the

---

12. www.cultuurnet.be. Accessed in December 2009.

cultural policy objectives of Georgia. In Poland, the principles of state cultural policy from 1993 list cultural democracy and the role of civil society among the main principles. Emphasis is also put on the decentralisation of cultural administration, which gives considerable decision-making powers to local authorities – this is also mentioned in the constitution (Article 15). The 1998 policy priority list included the democratisation of culture by eliminating differences between high and popular culture and, interestingly, a quest for space for family-oriented participation in culture. The 2003 priorities included access to cultural goods and the 2005 long list of guidelines comprised actions to foster the participation of young people. The list for national operational cultural programmes for 2006 included initiatives to allow young people to access and participate in culture and strengthen participation in general through infrastructural changes.

In Moldova, the Development and Protection of Culture and the Arts aims at ensuring access to national and international cultural values and support for citizens' cultural activities. The Czech Republic's 2001 cultural policy principles guarantee equality of access to cultural treasures, to facilitate access to disadvantaged social groups, and a specific aim "to support the widest possible involvement of citizens and civic initiatives in cultural and artistic activities, enhance their access to cultural values and participation in the care of cultural heritage, including their active and fully-fledged participation in decision-making procedures".

Lithuania's cultural policy programme for 2001-04 and that for 2004-06 listed expanding democracy in cultural life, and developing the information society and access to culture as themes for government action. As regards participation in regional cultural events and actions, the *Principles of Lithuanian cultural policy* (2001) and the *Regional culture development programme* (2003) listed measures for equal access to culture and participation in cultural life.

In Estonia, the ministry of culture's Development Plan 2007-10 lists concern for participation in cultural life as one of the themes of Estonian cultural policy. Among the current cultural policy priorities, there are several points referring to access and participation, including support for the cultural autonomy of ethnic minorities living in Estonia; an increase in the opportunities for all members of society to participate in cultural decision making; popular participation in amateur activities; and means to enable the public to keep in touch with professional culture.

The National Development Plan for the Cultural Sector 2007-13 for Romania regards culture and access to culture as rights, and social cohesion and the right to culture as important thematic areas for cultural policy.

The Romanian Government Directive 78/2005 sets cultural freedom – one of the guiding principles of the ministry of culture and religious affairs – as the essence of progress and development, and underlines the importance of culture for the quality of life and social cohesion. Based on this, some of the government's objectives are to:

– increase the degree of access to and participation in culture;
– promote creativity and participation in cultural life;
– promote diversity and the preservation of cultural identities;
– protect multiculturalism;
– foster cultural life within local communities;
– support community involvement in the development of the knowledge society, through promoting universal access by public institutions to information centres.

In many European countries, policy reflects the Council of Europe's general cultural objectives, which include promotion of identity, diversity, support of creativity and participation in cultural life. One of the most visible ways to strengthen participation in cultural life is through education, whether at school or outside. In today's Europe, lifelong learning and its relation to culture are manifested through "citizen education" and awareness-raising. Learning and education processes incorporate elements related to cultural rights since they imply equality between citizens, intercultural comprehension, expression and creativity as well as artistic practice. Education for the citizen is carried out through various activities (awareness-raising campaigns, neighbourhood community development, cultural work) and in actions against social exclusion. The contribution of non-governmental associations, particularly cultural ones, is fundamental for the delivery of lifelong learning programmes.

The socio-political objectives of Austrian cultural policy include elements such as participation, equality and representation, as is the case with Malta's cultural policy document (2001). The latter lists accessibility for all citizens to allow them to participate in cultural life (including socially disadvantaged communities and minority cultural groups). In 2002, the act that established the Maltese Council for Culture and the Arts includes the objective of increasing accessibility for all to arts and cultural initiatives. Likewise the Lithuanian cultural policy objectives expressed in the *Principles of Lithuanian cultural policy* (2001) and *The strategic plan of the ministry of culture for the period 2006-08* list the guarantee of participation in cultural life and consumption of culture as one of the main topics. Participation in cultural life in Lithuania is "oriented towards accessibility and the creation of conditions for society and communities to take part in various forms of cultural activities".[13]

Ensuring access and participation is understood frequently as promising financial resources (budgetary allocations), promoting social cohesion or fostering physical access to cultural institutions and services.

According to Greek cultural policy, access and participation are dealt with through investments and infrastructure, educational policies and free access to museums and archaeological sites: "promotion of equal access to and participation in cultural life for citizens of all regions, through the development of cultural institutions, adequate infrastructure and operational programmes of cultural activities at the local level. Recently, the emphasis has been to improve cultural provision and encourage access and participation through linking existing networks of cultural institutions, mainly via the Domain of Culture network of networks."[14]

Icelandic cultural policy for 2007 stipulated that "state support of the arts and culture is meant to allow Icelandic citizens to enjoy arts and culture regardless of their social status and to ensure a favourable working environment for artists".[15] The Romanian National Development Plan for the Cultural Sector 2007-13 also recognises support for activities that are geared towards participation.

In France, the ministry of culture carried out a project in 1996-97 called Cultural Projects in the Neighbourhood, which consisted of artists' input to the fight against discrimination. The impact of these experiences was evaluated through a study to help understand the synergy between artists and the urban population. In 1998, 4 million French people used the so-called "vacation cheques", and 400 000 of whom used them in at least one of the 4 000 cultural venues included in the scheme. France also offered a service of "personalised cheques of accompaniment" to enable people with difficulties to have access to cultural goods or services. There is also a "bonus" system for young people to buy books. In 2000, 40 000 young people benefited from this scheme. The French Social Cohesion Plan (2005) includes access to the arts, culture and artistic practice. In Finland, the culture voucher committee has proposed changes to the Income Tax Act to provide an exemption for an employee's chosen cultural activity, which the employer financially

13. Compendium country report on Lithuania (2006).
14. Compendium report on Greece.
15. "Culture", 2007. Available at http://bella.mrn.stjr.is/utgafur/culture_2007.pdf. Accessed in December 2009.

supports. At the moment the voucher system covers recreational and sporting activities although the committee proposed enlarging this system to include cultural activities.

In Swedish cultural policies, cultural rights have had a central role for a long time. The priorities of state cultural policies, established in 1974 (updated in 1996), include many elements of international instruments related to human and cultural rights. These priorities form the basis of the national cultural administration's work and mark priorities for programmes to be financed. According to the ministry of culture, these priorities currently include the requirements to:

– safeguard freedom of expression and create genuine opportunities for everyone to make use of that freedom;
– take action to enable everyone to participate in cultural life, to experience culture, and to engage in creative activities of their own;
– promote cultural diversity, artistic renewal and quality, thereby counteracting the negative effects of commercialism;
– enable culture to act as a dynamic, challenging and independent force in society;
– preserve and make use of the cultural heritage;
– promote cultural education; and
– promote international cultural exchange and meetings between different cultures in Sweden.

In recent years, Swedish cultural policy has contained a strong element of cultural diversity and inclusion through culture and media. The Swedish Arts Council lists as the main objective of Swedish cultural policy "to increase access for all who live in Sweden to culture, both via contact with culture of high quality and through creative activity of their own". 2006 was declared the Year of Cultural Diversity in order to reflect this objective and to increase permanently the opportunities of all people living in Sweden to participate in cultural life and create links between different cultural traditions. Another objective was to create incentives so that cultural activities could reflect and incorporate the ethnic and cultural diversity that exists in Sweden. Extra resources of 3 million Swedish krona (SEK) (€331 000) were allocated by the Swedish Arts Council to a number of applications which totalled SEK 50 million (€5.5 million). The resources granted to various institutions are mainly focused on children, diversity, people with disabilities and gender equality activities. The institutions that receive funding are required once a year to report on how they have taken these groups into account with regard to their public, personnel and content. The year 2007 was declared the Year of Young People and Children.

Another state that planned to enhance access for young people and children was the United Kingdom. It cited the rights of children to "develop their talents to the full and enjoy the benefits of participation". In the UK, access has been one of the priority issues since the 1980s. This principle has been translated into cultural policy priorities through the plans of the Arts Councils (originally of the Arts Council of Great Britain, later divided between the UK's constituent nations). More recently the Scottish Executive Agency has published a report (2009) on the Pathfinder Programme – a programme of 13 projects supported by the Scottish Government (2006-08) and run by local authorities to explore effective and practical ways to get people involved in cultural activity. The Welsh Assembly's 10-year culture strategy outlined as priority issues the inclusion of culture as part of local community plans; free entry to national museums and galleries and improving access to cultural facilities and activities for audiences and participants. Likewise in Northern Ireland, the principle of increasing opportunities to participate in the arts was included in the five-year Arts Plan from 2001 to 2006.

In 1998, the Future Committee of the Finnish Parliament presented a report that affirms amongst its conclusions that together with economic and technological elements, humanity needs a culturally sustainable basis of global ethics. The Strategic Plan of the Finnish Government from 2000 affirms in Chapter 6 (Cultural, sport and youth policies), with regard to the social impact of policies, that "the impacts in the society of the objectives of cultural and art policies of the Ministry of Education and Culture are based at the national and international level on three pillars: creativity, cultural diversity and equality. Cultural policies have an important impact on the realisation of welfare, regional development and innovation policies."[16] The objectives included the promotion of access to art, culture and information as well as the promotion of cultural rights and participation. The recommended actions relating to access, cultural rights and participation included the following steps: to improve diversity of the culture offered, artistic and cultural exchange, as well as cultural information and the accessibility of cultural and artistic information; the egalitarian realisation of cultural rights; to reflect the demographic change of the population in the design of artistic and cultural services; to promote sustainable cultural development; and to improve the accessibility of arts and culture as well as the participation of ethnic groups and disabled people.

In other countries as well, access to cultural institutions has been the subject of policies addressing cultural participation. Access to museums is a visible act and many other countries have adopted initiatives of free entrance on a regular basis.

16. Tulossuunnitelma (2006).

In Estonia public museums can be visited for free once a month and in Austria specific projects (such as the Long Night of Museums) have been created to successfully attract more people to museums. The cultural policy of Luxembourg also includes the revision of opening hours of cultural institutions and actions to attract a new public, and work in collaboration with different artists and institutions in order to carry out activities that raise the public's awareness of culture.

The Swedish Arts Council allocates grants to the Culture in Work Life programme (*Kultur i arbetslivet*), with the idea that the workplace may play an important role in the enjoyment of and access to culture – and that cultural activities may have a positive impact on a person's work performance and general health. The programme aims at stimulating cultural activities through labour unions. Fostering access to and participation in cultural life is included in the design and curricula of art and culture institutions. Accessibility is reflected in Sweden's policy that entrance to public museums should be free. This move was led by the museums, such as the Moderna Museet (Museum of Contemporary Art), Swedish Museum of Architecture and the Museum of Antiquity. In 2005, the scheme was enlarged to include most public museums, though in 2006 this initiative was restricted to young people under 20.

In a similar way, the Norwegian Council for Cultural Affairs provides support to projects that aim at conserving the Norwegian cultural heritage and making it accessible for all. The status of minority culture is considered equal to ethnic Norwegian cultural heritage. In Denmark, entrance to all officially recognised museums is free for children and young people. In Poland, a Law on Museums (1996) guarantees free admission to museums one day per week and reduced ticket prices. In Latvia as well, museums offer free admission once a week. In France, since 2000, 33 national museums offer free admission one Sunday a month and free entrance to young people under 18. In 2007, the French Ministry of Culture announced a new programme of free admission to museums.

Many countries offer entrance to cultural institutions at concessionary cost. This is usually the case for young people, senior citizens and in some countries people with disabilities.

In San Marino, in the At the Theatre in the Balcony project (2006/07), run by the Office for Cultural and Social Activities, theatre is made available for all through reduced ticket prices. In the Netherlands, there are several measures for facilitating access to cultural institutions through discounts and special cards; mainly aimed at young people and people with low income.

Ensuring the dissemination of culture to the national population is a cultural policy objective in most countries.

In Norway, this principle translates into programmes such as the Cultural Rucksack (*den kulturelle skolesekken* – launched in 2001), which aims to ensure that students of primary and lower secondary schools have access to the enjoyment of cultural experiences, expression and creativity in various arts disciplines.[17] Also, the policies addressed to the Sami population emphasise the fostering of their cultural activities (see 5.4).

In the Netherlands, the Cultural Outreach Plan of 2000 had as an objective the involvement of more people in cultural life, especially immigrants and young people. Cultural activities in the plan are understood in a broad sense to include youth culture and popular culture. The central government and the provinces and municipalities set up an agreement on programmes for the period between 2001 and 2004. The success of the plan secured an extension for four years. Actions within the plan include the following instruction: "improve programming; create more space for cultural diversity; invest in young people to enable them to participate in a diversified cultural life actively; obtain better visibility of cultural assets; and create optional conditions for culture-based urban and rural planning".[18]

Decentralisation of cultural administration is one way to foster democratisation of culture.

In Slovenia, the democratisation of culture had already started in the 1980s, but no cultural policy principles were set out before the National Programme for Culture 2004-07, which gives local governments the possibility of defining their own cultural priorities. Local support for cultural activities and participation is important and municipalities with a high proportion of national minorities are required to support their cultural activities. The Public Interest in Culture Act of 2002 includes access to culture and active cultural participation in cultural life as policy objectives.

In Finland, the decentralisation of cultural administration is an important step in fostering participation in cultural life throughout the country. The 2015 Strategy Plan of the ministry of education and culture lists as key functions, amongst others, safeguarding equal access to education and culture and enhancing opportunities for sharing and participation. Also, in 2005 the minister for culture launched a programme on

17. More at www.denkulturelleskolesekken.no/oversettelser/english.htm. Accessed in December 2009.
18. Compendium report on the Netherlands.

the ethnic dimension of cultural policies under the title "Fair Culture", which includes a series of participatory actions as well as ethical planning for future cultural policies.

While many countries have listed access to and participation in culture as priority issues, there is still a lack of political commitment, concrete programmes and use of tools that can be considered to be real and adequate indicators.

A rights-based approach to cultural policy places emphasis on promoting and strengthening ways to provide broader access for the entire population and encourages public awareness of the importance of the protection and promotion of the diversity of cultural identity and diversity.

Policies to protect cultural rights share common features regardless of the specific cultural context, as the examples below illustrate. They all:

Recognise *the diversity of cultural expressions as an important factor that allows individuals and communities to express and share their ideas, beliefs and values and as an important source of intangible and material wealth*

Promote *plurality of identities and cultural expressions of diverse cultures by taking into account that culture takes diverse forms across time and location*

Incorporate *international instruments that promote the free flow of ideas through the arts and use culture and cultural expressions as a strategic element in national and international development policy*

Provide *an environment that celebrates the importance and protects cultural diversity as a fundamental freedom as proclaimed in the Universal Declaration of Human Rights*

Enable interaction and the free flow of ideas experienced through cultural diversity through the nurture of constant changes and interactions between cultures

Protect *the intellectual property rights in sustaining those involved in cultural creativity*

Engelhardt 2006

Access to information and modern technologies is one form of ensuring people's participation in culture, even though they may not be traditional forms of such. Wi-Fi and social networking spaces are increasingly available and on many citizens' wish list, as is the provision of schools with computers and Internet access.

Many governments, such as the Maltese, offer free e-mail addresses to all their citizens. Mobile phone content is opening up fresh opportunities, especially to the young. There is already an argument that says access to the Internet is as much a cultural right as access to libraries was in the last century. And there are still many Europeans for whom access is difficult. In Sweden, the portal Culturenet Sweden (www.kultur.nu/index.asp) is a virtual gateway to facilitate access to Swedish culture through the Internet. The portal, maintained by the Swedish Arts Council, has 8 175 links to Swedish culture at local and national level and from a variety of cultural providers. In October 2009, Finland became the first country in the world to declare broadband Internet access a legal right.

Some European countries have included the concept of cultural rights or access to cultural life in their policies on development aid.

This is the case in Spain, which has included cultural rights within the Strategic Action Plan for International Cooperation for Development on culture and development. One of Spain's initiatives in Europe is to collaborate in the launch of a library for blind people in Sarajevo. With the National Organisation of Blind People in Spain helping to record texts in Braille, Spain is contributing works of Spanish literature that have been translated into other languages.

Several European countries have programmes or institutions to promote or assist national diaspora communities. These initiatives tend to help nationals living abroad to be connected with the national culture at home and to maintain linguistic skills. However, these activities or cultural centres can function as a true channel of participation in cultural life. They implement educational, cultural, social and community activities and help to maintain connections with national cultures as well as facilitate access to culture for foreign nationals.

Some other countries are gradually adapting policies and programmes to pay closer attention to participation and access.

The Ministry of Culture and Tourism of Azerbaijan initiated programmes in 2007 to make culture accessible to people from different social groups. These actions are carried out mainly by offering access to museums and monuments.

Despite all this, there are still a number of countries that have not yet adopted specific policies as regards the participation of the general public in cultural life, or linking social cohesion with culture. This is the case, for example, in Albania, Ukraine, Bulgaria, San Marino and "the former Yugoslav Republic of Macedonia". In other countries, such as Denmark, access to cultural life is not linked to other sociocultural frameworks such as citizenship or social cohesion. Furthermore, although in some countries participation in cultural life is acknowledged in cultural policy, it is hardly translated into effective policies. This is the case, for example, in Croatia, Georgia, Moldova and the Russian Federation, even if some initiatives related to vulnerable groups exist. In other countries, there are no specific programmes on participation and cultural citizenship, but local administrations are required to answer the cultural needs of the inhabitants. This is the case, for example, in Slovenia.

The pattern across Europe is uneven. The Council of Europe's cultural compendium report on Italy acknowledges that there too there is a lack of a national policy relating to participation in cultural life and existing inequalities in access to culture, as well as the role of culture in social cohesion. The existing examples at the national level are mainly ornamental; however, at the local level, activities run by cultural and social agencies and associations are various and effective.

3.3 Surveying cultural access, participation, provision and rights

Most European countries carry out surveys on cultural participation, which usually entail studies of attendance at cultural institutions and the use of other cultural services. A number of these surveys seek to evaluate the effects of policies aimed at cultural democratisation. Through surveys, systems of cultural indicators and cultural statistics, the aim is to measure the influence of public intervention.

In methodological terms, the national and international surveys share similar operational models when it comes to selecting population samples, but there are variations among surveys in the constitution and contents of the samples. Most of the work on national cultural policies and participation has been carried out on behalf of and financed by the public authorities. However, in recent years cultural institutions have been encouraged to carry out their own surveys.

UNESCO launched its New Framework for Cultural Statistics in 2009.[19] In Europe, general figures on cultural attendance and participation can be sourced in the cultural statistics compiled by Eurostat, the statistical office of the European Union, the cultural participation figures provided by ERICarts and, at state level, the compendium country profiles that present cultural policies and figures in member states of the Council of Europe (see: www.culturalpolicies.net). The compendium functions as a centre for resources on cultural policies and tendencies as regards participation in cultural life. The authors distinguish between attendance at cultural activities that receive public subsidies and "consumption" of cultural activities, goods and services.

In 1995, the European ministries of culture adopted a resolution on the promotion of statistical information in the field of culture and economic growth.[20] The first problem in a comparison of levels of access and participation is the disparity and divergence in the definitions of the cultural field and its structure, and the statistical methods of each country. In order to generate comparable statistics, the European Union created a leadership group on culture within Eurostat and in 2000 a working group was established. The group, in charge of drafting a survey on participation in cultural life, presented its findings in 2002.

The 2001 Eurobarometer survey of Europeans' participation in cultural activities (Eurobarometer 2002) shows in general figures the cultural participation trends of member states. The results showed that, while northern Europeans read more than southern Europeans, the major element in cultural participation relates to watching television. Whether this can really be regarded as participation is debatable. At that time, more than half of Europeans did not use a computer, though this is likely to have changed significantly since 2001. The survey also shows that libraries and cinemas are the most frequented places for cultural attendance. Less than one in ten respondents found no obstacles to participating in cultural life, meaning that the vast majority of people feel that they have difficulties in fulfilling their cultural needs. The first obstacle mentioned is time, followed by price, lack of interest and information, poor quality of culture on offer and lack of cultural education. According to the study, 82% of Europeans see free access to culture as a positive element that favours participation.

19. See www.uis.unesco.org/template/pdf/cscl/framework/FCS_2009_EN.pdf. Participation is divided into home-based, going out and identity-building.
20. Council resolution of 20 November 1995 on the promotion of statistics on culture and economic growth (95/C 327/01), European Union.

The Michail Skaliotis paper, "Key figures on cultural participation in the European Union" (2002), presents the results obtained in the analysis of the 2001 Eurobarometer survey and acknowledges the lack of a harmonised statistical framework in Europe. According to Skaliotis, the Eurobarometer survey was the first one to offer comparable data on cultural participation in European countries.

In 2003 Eurobarometer carried out a study on new Europeans and culture, in order to analyse some of the key elements related to culture as experienced by the general public of 13 candidate countries. One of the results of the study was that the majority of the then future European Union citizens thought at the time that responsibility for culture should be dealt with at national level. As for studying participation in Europe over a longer period, the Council of Europe's National Cultural Policy Review Programme has been providing interesting findings since 1960. More recent studies include subsequent comparisons based on the information gathered from different countries by CIRCLE (Cultural Information and Research Centres Liaison in Europe), the "Eurostat pocketbook on cultural statistics" (2007), which shows interesting statistics on cultural participation, and the 2009 study on access of young people to culture, by the Interarts Foundation commissioned by the Youth Unit of the Education, Audiovisual and Culture Executive Agency of the European Commission.

Countries conduct participation studies with varying frequency. The French Ministry of Culture studies cultural practices every eight years, the Netherlands every four years and Spain and Italy more often. Sometimes, two different studies in the same setting provide different results, a discrepancy which often raises questions about their accuracy. There has been continuing criticism of data gathering in Europe and calls to update national systems. There is a clear need to develop new systems for monitoring and evaluating participation policies at the European level.

Although the initial objective was to evaluate participation in certain limited areas of culture, research fields have developed into analysis of social and cultural change. Emilie Vidal underlines in a mapping exercise prepared for this study that "for example, in recent surveys what is taken into account is the different types of shows, and forms of "amateur" and associative activities. This evolution reflects the growing extension of the concept of culture itself with the acknowledgment of the role of media and popular cultures that have placed a necessity to adapt cultural surveys into the new situation. For example, the study on the consumption of products of cultural industries by the Department of Studies, Future Trends and Statistics (DEPS) in France surveys the consumption of French cultural products and services between 1995 and 2004 (book editing, videos, movies, television, shows, expenditure on audiovisual programmes, etc.)."[21] According to Gilles Pronovost, studying cultural activities allows us to emphasise the structure of behaviour and social processes that function in all societies, such as social stratification and stereotypes. In 2007, the French Department of Culture published a new edition of Key Statistics that deals with a large selection of cultural sectors according to a transversal approach to the great themes of cultural policies (employment, financing, practices).

According to the 2004 study of the European Foundation for the Improvement of Living and Working Conditions on the perceptions of the quality of life in greater Europe, "access to social and cultural activities" was considered of minor importance. According to that study, all Europeans share a similar view of what constitutes a good life; "being in good health", having sufficient income, a good family life and social relations are the main elements for enjoying a high quality of lifestyle. The "Eurostat pocketbook on cultural statistics" from 2007 recalls that most cultural activities (especially related to art) still tend to be the pastime of a small proportion of the population and that there is a strong correlation between financial and educational status and cultural participation. It also shows differences between women and men in cultural participation, even if men have more leisure time. The overview shows, too, differences between countries in Internet use and broadband connection as well as in time spent on cultural activities.

In 2007, *Cultural Trends* published J. Mark Schuster's study "Participation studies and cross-national comparison: proliferation, prudence and possibility", an overview of 20 participation studies in 35 states. In it he said that "participation studies have implications that go well beyond the arena of good statistical practice". His study, however, concentrates on what he calls "traditional" participation studies, which means studies that can be summarised as a participation rate of the adult population in a given country. Schuster acknowledges that, for example, most of the audience surveys sample visits rather than visitors.

21. "The consumption of cultural industry products" (April 2006), Department of Studies, Future Trends and Statistics, French Ministry of Culture, document disseminated together with "The expenditure of families on culture-media in 2001, available at www.culture.gouv.fr and www2.culture.gouv.fr/culture/deps/2008/pdf/Cchiffres_06.pdf.

However, he suggested that, "the interest in participation studies has been accelerated by an increased government emphasis on planning, evaluation, and accountability – in other words, the rise of cultural policy itself". He indicates that states are rebuilding their research capabilities and transnational governmental organisations are calling for comparative research even though the "driving force for cultural statistics will remain mainly national; this, in turn, works against the aspiration for comparability". Schuster points out that although many experts doubt the meaningfulness of comparative cultural statistics, especially when countries have such different cultural traditions, he also argues that such comparative statistics can be useful in drawing general international trends.

Schuster found that studies are not designed in the same way, they are not initiated for the same reason, they do not serve the same principles and sometimes they do not even ask the same questions or understand "participation" in the same way. Schuster cites McCarthy and Jinnett (2001) who conclude that the whos, whats and hows of participation are frequently examined more in studies than the whys. Schuster also cites Huysmans, van den Broek and de Haan (2005) when he indicates that the gender difference in receptive participation is greatest in performing arts and art forms related to cultural canons, and less noticeable in cabaret and pop music – but it is more difficult to examine people's motivations when it comes to participation. He notes that participation studies that show obstacles to cultural participation "are likely to estimate unsatisfied demand for particular art forms and particular cultural experiences".

In the United Kingdom, Arts Council England commissioned the Office for National Statistics (ONS) to survey attendance, participation and attitudes to the arts. This survey has been carried out several times, and according to the comparison of the results from 2001 and 2003, access to the Internet may foster participation, as a growing number of people book tickets or find information about arts events online. A participation survey from 2007 by the Department for Culture, Media and Sport (DCMS) found that 94% of adults living in England participated in at least one cultural activity in 2006. Similar kinds of studies have been carried out, for example, in Bulgaria (cultural attitudes and consumption of cultural products in Bulgaria, 2005), Estonia (the culture consuming survey, 2003), Finland (yearly statistics), France ("les pratiques culturelles des Français"), Germany, Italy (statistics by the Istituto Nazionale di Statistica), Ireland, Latvia (culture consumption in Latvia, 2007) and Malta (cultural statistics, 2004; theatregoers, 2003), among others. The studies mentioned represent only a sample of existing studies.

Participation studies provide information not only about attendance and participation, but also about a lack of such activity. This is the case for studies from Austria, where participation in culture is fairly low and as much as 70% of the population claimed that they had not visited a theatre or museum or attended a concert in the previous year. The example highlights that it is not the same to study attendance at theatres and museums, and activities related to heritage, home-based cultural activities, participation through new technologies or cultural "curiosities".

Europe seems also to be divided into active and non-active cultural consumers. Although many studies distinguish between different ethnic and social groups (even if defining a "social group" is difficult) and gender, there are results that indicate differences in participation and consumption between social groups.

> In Estonia, even where – by international comparison – the participation rate of people remains generally very high, elderly people and national minorities are more alienated from cultural life than others. But this seems not to be the case, for example, in Romania, where a survey of trends between 1998 and 2003 showed no significant differences between ethnic groups with the exception of the Roma. At the 1991 CIRCLE (Cultural Information and Research Centres Liaison in Europe) round table on participation studies, it was said that similar kinds of cultural pursuits practised by a similar number of people can have completely different outcomes and, conversely, attendance at quite different cultural forms can have similar kinds of results.

Bina (2006) makes reference to the fact that research on cultural participation shows a link with the level of education. He notes that education is also an important prerequisite for access to culture, especially if access is understood as meaning access to cultural services. This is a trend that comes out in many surveys. Another is that in many European countries participation in new cultural forms and popular culture is quite strong, while participation in traditional forms of culture may not be declining, but is fairly constant.

> The 2005 study on "culture lovers" and "culture leavers" in the Netherlands underlines this. It also suggests that performing arts and music audiences are growing older while at the same time there is growing participation by children in cultural activities. The study includes an interesting chapter on cultural participation at home, even though the most common form of cultural participation at home remains watching television. This study also shows differences in the participation of different ethnic groups and their preferences in art and other forms of culture.

In 2005, the Social and Cultural Planning Office conducted a survey on the cultural participation and media habits of ethnic groups in the Netherlands and the results were published in 2007 in the report "Comparing cultural practices: content and context of cultural activities of ethnic groups in the Netherlands". It was shown that opportunities for participation in cultural life are concentrated in the major cities and that ethnic minorities clearly participate less in cultural life than other groups, even though their participation is slowly rising. This study showed similar results to earlier ones but observed that there are generational differences within ethnic groups. Second generation people from minorities tend to be already strongly integrated in Dutch society. There were also differences to some extent between cultural groups, but recently the gaps have been shrinking.

In France, according to a 2005 Observatory of Inequalities,[22] despite all the efforts to democratise cultural life, attendance at cultural events varies according to social class. Some 50% of those questioned in professional classes attended a show while only 22% of the working class did so. According to this study, the differences are greatest in theatre attendance and reading.

As regards participation, studies on barriers to participation give some guidance on people's policy expectations. In 2004, the association Cemaforre[23] carried out a survey in France on the accessibility of performing arts. The report shows that few people with disabilities attend theatres, with the exception of elderly people who might have problems with hearing, vision or mobility. The survey showed that most of the organisations had no special physically adapted access. In Spain, obstacles to cultural participation were mainly found in the price of entrance tickets, the lack of attractive opportunities on offer and elderly peoples' difficulties in going out. In the 2003 survey by Arts Council England, the most frequent barriers were difficulties in finding time and the cost of activities. The results indicate that people in "managerial and professional groups were most likely to mention lack of time as a factor in not attending more events (59% compared with less than 48% of all other socio-economic groups)". The study also shows that there was a difference in the perception of barriers between those who wished to attend more and those who did not. The ones wanting to attend hoped to have more time to do so and those that planned not to attend cited the lack of interest as the obstacle. According to this study, people in general think that the arts perform an important role in society, cultural projects should receive public funding and that it is important to ensure schoolchildren's access to and participation in arts and culture. As in other countries, the study shows regional differences in attendance.

---

22. www.inegalites.fr/.
23. A French association to develop and promote access to culture and leisure for everyone, especially people with disabilities. The association chairs EUCREA International, an NGO for the promotion of access of people with disabilities to culture and media. More information at: www.cemaforre.asso.fr.

Participation studies also reveal a new understanding of cultural participation that might differ from participation in the arts, but emphasises participation in popular culture.

In Malta, the 2006 survey by the National Office of Statistics shows very low attendance at theatres, probably due to high entrance costs. Other surveys show that even if Malta has low attendance levels at cultural institutions, public celebrations have a strong presence in the Maltese cultural calendar.

At times, participation studies try to reflect the opinions and feelings of the respondents.

In a 2004 study of the cultural demands of Lithuanian people, a large portion (41%) of the respondents believed that cultural education and activities foster integration of young people and social groups in danger of isolation. Young people and people with higher education were identified as most active in cultural participation. The study also identified festivals, concerts and art fairs as the most popular cultural events and called for more cultural services for those living in rural areas. A 2005 study in Bulgaria found that participation in traditional forms of culture is declining due to new forms taking their place. According to this study, only 1.4% of the population attended theatre, movies, opera, ballet or museums. The results of the study also show that sociocultural factors and education are important in participation and that traditional cultural forms are not reaching the public. "People from my social environment do not visit these places"[24] was an example of one of the most cited arguments.

In 2003, the opinion research company MORI carried out a study on the impact of free entry to museums in the UK. The study revealed that not only had attendance risen by 10% but that people planned to donate more when visiting and were more likely to pay entrance fees to those special exhibitions for which there was still a charge.

The 2006 study of public participation in the arts in Ireland shows that citizens in general are in favour of fostering participation and financial support given to activities that strengthen participation, especially that of children and young people. The respondents also favoured actions that facilitate participation in expression and creation at the local level, for example, through amateur and community-based arts and programmes. The study highlights the importance given to the visibility of arts that reflect the multicultural

73

24. Compendium report on Bulgaria.

nature of contemporary Irish society. It also stated that access to arts and culture was easier than it had been 10 years before, thanks to financial investment and better infrastructure.

The Interarts study (2004) on local and regional perspectives on cultural rights and the right to take part in cultural life showed that people in general do not have great faith in legal standards. The main elements of the right to participate in cultural life are considered to be: equal opportunities ensured by local authorities; the right of the individual to participate in culture; the rights of minorities and indigenous people to maintain cultural autonomy; economic access to cultural services and sites; preservation of national and international cultural heritage; and a responsibility to protect minorities, indigenous peoples and other vulnerable groups and the use of minority languages.

As expected, there is a gender difference in attending cultural activities. For example, in Sweden where people are fairly engaged in participating in cultural activities, women are more likely to participate than men. Studies in Sweden also show a general increase in participation in new forms of cultural content and activities, and that Swedes are more active in participating than in producing culture. In Spain, participation in or attendance at cultural activities is clearly stronger in some areas of the country than in others. Southern Europeans in general tend to go to the movies more and read less than northern Europeans.

In several countries there have been attempts to establish certain basic ethical elements in cultural policies and basic criteria for cultural rights. The examples of Scotland and Finland are set out below in more detail. An interesting process was carried out in Ukraine. In 2004, a group of Ukrainian experts, representatives of cultural organisations and the parliament's committee on culture proposed the development of a set of basic standards for cultural services that the state should promote, provide and guarantee, especially at the local level. In 2006, an inter-ministerial working group was established. The main themes were "how to determine core services demanded by a local community (in other words, how to make them flexible) and how to measure their impact".[25]

Mark Schuster warned against the dangers of comparing participation data from different countries. He pointed out that, "the broad nature of existing participation questions, due to the need for relatively short

---

25. Butsenko (2006).

surveys that remain consistent over time, does not provide the rich policy detail necessary for assessment, evaluation, and policy reform". He suggested that, in order to understand cultural participation and to translate statistical data into policies, the state administration should seek the support of researchers and analysts. He also suggested that instead of stressing cultural participation – where everyone would have their own form of cultural engagement and access (everyone could choose to engage in a form of cultural practice if they so wish) – one might need to consider an enlargement of the definition of culture. It is, then, in the changing cultural practices of the adult population that one could find traces of a new meaning for cultural participation.

3.4 Cultural citizenship and participation

Participation is strongly linked to cultural citizenship. The very concept of civil society is linked to the promotion and protection of cultural rights and freedoms. Many of the cultural activists' organisations in civil society were "born" promoting and protecting cultural identities and collective rights. Although citizenship is above all a political or social concept, it has also gained a strong cultural content as well. Many sources claim that cultural citizenship is closely linked to the idea of feeling part of a community and that without the fulfilment of cultural citizenship it is not possible to develop a cohesive community.

Dick Stanley says in his publication *A reflection on the function of culture in building citizenship capacity* (2007) that, "the cultural participation of citizens functions as a form of continuous education as well as an ongoing negotiation of collective solutions to the contingencies of life. Members of a society who are excluded from this continuous education and ongoing negotiation are thereby prevented from exercising full citizenship." John Foote (2006) states that cultural citizenship includes "respect for diversity, fundamental democratic values, a shared but often divergent history and heritage, and an ongoing contribution to peaceful intercultural dialogue and relations".

Patrice Meyer-Bisch establishes a strong link between democracy and cultural rights. According to him the development of cultural liberties is an acknowledgement of the dignity of everyone. Cultural rights are fundamental factors of democratisation because they ensure the conservation and valuing of diversity and the development of cultural richness. He also argues that placing cultural rights at the centre of policies is one of the conditions for participatory democracy, since they foster the effective participation of everyone in the public debate.

In general, the institutional framework of responsibility for cultural policies suggests the primacy of the public (especially governmental) sphere. Awareness within civil society of the chance to participate in decisions on the management of national cultural heritage is a relatively recent phenomenon. The weakness of civil society is mostly due to low levels of participation and limited inter-relations among civil society actors. However, European civil society in culture is undergoing a process of reorganisation and is strengthening its ability to mobilise resources in order to have its say. The role of the civil society is indispensable in assuring dignified life conditions for everyone.

An important part of creative and expressive cultural participation takes place in local cultural centres and through amateur or voluntary activities. Participation is closely related to the idea of social cohesion. It is often demonstrated that the weaker the "feeling" of social cohesion is in a community, the lower the access and the sense of engagement. In 2004, the University of Northumbria published a "Report of a thematic study using transnational comparisons to analyse and identify cultural policies and programmes that contribute to preventing and reducing poverty and social exclusion". The aim of the study was to research the impact of access to and participation in cultural activities in combating poverty and social exclusion in eight selected countries. The findings of the study showed that most of the countries identify certain disadvantaged groups as those most at risk of exclusion, but there were no cohesive programmes at national level that link culture and social inclusion. The report also showed that there was a relative lack of knowledge on the positive role of culture, and underlined the negative impact of limited funding and short-term targets. As part of the recommendations, the study proposed producing a set of indicators to measure the impact of participation in cultural activities on social exclusion.

However, strong participation in civil society movements, such as those related to the environment or human rights, do not necessarily translate into the same enthusiastic activity in the case of cultural rights and participation in cultural life. As George Yúdice (2006) puts it: "There is very little public awareness of the importance of cultural rights and cultural diversity among not only the populace but also the legislators and journalists of just about any country. There are several reasons for this, but I think two are major: the construction of newsworthiness and the lack of citizen mobilisation." Although the cultural sector is a field where voluntary action and strong feelings on the importance of culture for the well-being of people are driving forces, there has not been a similar kind of independent organisational initiative as in the environmental and human rights sectors.

Furthermore Yúdice states that, "successful mobilisation requires rallying around issues about which people are or can become passionate. Some of the issues broached in the documents on cultural rights and diversity are quite abstract or distant. It is hard to imagine activists breaking into legislative meetings or corporative offices over social cohesion, values and meaning, intercultural dialogue, or international cooperation." Yúdice calls for civil society activism on cultural rights and presents as an example the mobilisation in Mexico in favour of the Mexican cinema versus US-owned distribution circuits.

A large portion of cultural provision is carried out through voluntary, non-profit or other third sector organisations. In most countries, public administration offers support to civil society organisations even though, according to Dorota Ilczuk's 2001 study on the synergies between cultural policies and the development of the civil society in nine European countries, there is considerable diversity in the perception and valuation of the role and impact of the third sector. One of the main factors in this is the historical development of the relationship between culture and civil society. There is also the concept of "cultural citizenship" that could be considered to be the grass-roots level. Cultural citizenship is about continuous education, reciprocity and participation, and includes issues such as freedom of creation, cultural recognition, the complexity of multiculturalism and the tension between cultural theory and the "praxis" of cultural institutions and daily life.

The report "In from the margins: a contribution to the debate on culture and development in Europe" (1997) of the Council of Europe stressed the importance of strengthening civil society and democracy through cultural measures. The report emphasised the role of culture in the search for creative answers to social problems, in safeguarding rights, as well in social cohesion. The report underlines the relationship between culture and civil society and acknowledges that, sometimes, voluntary action can be more appropriate in culture than government activity. There are several European networks and organisations that successfully advocate the role of civil society in the European cultural space. These include Culture Action Europe (the European Forum for the Arts and Heritage), the European Cultural Foundation, and CIRCLE, among others.

The civil society cultural sector is largely dependent on public funding. The third sector, often defined as the space of civil society separated from the public sector and market, responds to different functions within society. The third sector is an active arena for social cohesion, citizen education and different aspects of socio-ethics such as awareness-raising on various issues. Mestrovic (2004) states that, "the third sector is a space where many people learn for the first time to practice democratic participation" and Boccacin (2004) acknowledges that the third sector organisations deserve special attention for their "societal" role: a participatory means of social construction based on creation, care and the strengthening of community relationships. Some countries list close contacts with cultural NGOs among their cultural policy principles.

The reality, however, is often more ambivalent. In Romania studies on civic participation show that people have little trust in the public administration in general and the great majority of Romanians are not involved in non-governmental or voluntary work. Romania has a system of Rural Cultural Houses, but recently the level of cultural activity in these centres has been low.

> Studies in Ukraine show that cultural projects which aim at social cohesion are mainly run by civil society organisations and associations. The UK and Ireland channel the majority of their support for participation in arts through civil society organisations because the "arms-length principle" means that there are no wholly state-controlled delivery organisations. The results of the 2003 survey in the Republic of Karelia, Pskov and Novgorod *oblasts* of the Russian Federation show that the general public as well as policy makers do not see a link between culture and quality of life or social cohesion. However, another survey (VCIOM comparative survey) shows that the general public's call for active cultural revitalisation and cultural programming could facilitate social cohesion.

> In 2005 the Klon/Jawor Association carried out a study of the state of non-governmental organisations in Poland in 2004, which indicated that 11.5% (5 500) of Polish NGOs work in the field of art and culture. These organisations do not automatically animate participation in cultural life, but allow people to have contact with and access to many different fields of art and culture. The study also showed that most of the arts and culture NGOs work in urban environments and consist mainly of female activists.

Slovenia has approximately 4 000 cultural societies and associations that undertake work in the field of educational programmes for the elderly and young, together with different types of participation in art and cultural activities for both groups.

In Azerbaijan, the government prepared a State Programme on Poverty Reduction and Economic Development (SPPRED) in 2001 with the support of the World Bank and the International Monetary Fund. Different sectorial working groups including all governmental bodies drafted a final strategy in 2002 with programme lines on social cohesion and poverty reduction. The strategy was approved by a presidential decree in 2003 and included three cultural policy areas: stimulating cultural workers by increasing their professionalism and information provision; improvement of the capacities of cultural and arts institutions; and preserving cultural heritage to provide equitable use by the population at large and establish new cultural tourism roots to stimulate employment.

Traditionally, civil society has an active role in initiatives fostering social inclusion. In Austria, participation in the voluntary sector is high and many social inclusion and civil society organisations and cultural associations run access and culture projects locally. The same is true in Sweden, where the majority of the general public belong to associations – and of these roughly one fifth belong to the cultural sector. "Cultural associations are, therefore, important tools for a decentralised policy. They also have methods and contacts that are necessary to reach those parts of the population that do not usually participate in cultural activities. A general condition is that children's and young people's activities should be given priority."[26]

Arts Council England published a report in November 2007 entitled "Public value and the arts in England: discussion and conclusions of the arts debate". Its results emphasise the importance of arts in people's lives. "For many people the arts are a positive, happy but also challenging aspect of their lives. Participants described the social dimension as particularly important – people associate the arts with friendship, spending time with the family and sharing an experience with others from all walks of life."[27] The key findings of the process acknowledge that arts are seen as a fundamental part of people's capacity for life and sense of personal identity. Arts matter also because they add to the enrichment of experience and have

26. Compendium report on Sweden.
27. Bunting (2007), p. 8.

powerful application in other contexts such as education, social cohesion, emotional well-being, sharing experiences and economic growth. Interestingly, the respondents also felt that empowerment through arts and culture is valued more than access.[28] The report also suggested that even if people with little or no engagement in the arts or in cultural life placed little value on their own participation, practically everyone supports the idea of securing access for children to arts and culture. Arts Council England is taking these consultations into account in their short- and long-term planning.

The Interarts study from 2004 on local and regional understanding of cultural rights revealed that people in general have little faith in legal instruments and standards and their implementation in "real life" and the fulfilment of cultural rights. The study aimed at mapping people's needs in order to obtain a clearer picture of regional, local and individual perceptions of cultural rights and the right to take part in cultural life. According to this study the main elements are:

- equal opportunities ensured by local authorities;
- the right of the individual to participate in his/her culture;
- the rights of minorities and indigenous people to maintain their cultural autonomy;
- economic access to cultural services and sites;
- preservation of national and international cultural heritage;
- a responsibility to protect minorities, indigenous people and other vulnerable groups and their access to culture;
- use of minority languages.

Access and participation are fundamental elements of cultural rights and civil society. The enjoyment and fulfilment of cultural rights require an enabling environment and a legal framework that offer the bases for the protection of the rights related to cultural action, such as the right to participate in cultural life. As a consequence, democratic regularisation, capacity-building and an enabling environment are necessary for the construction, visibility and "maintenance" of a dynamic civil society.

---

28. "Indeed members of the public were clear that everyone can be uncomfortable about stepping out of their comfort zone, regardless of their particular financial, social or cultural background. As such the issue seems to be less about addressing the needs of specific groups and more about starting an inclusive conversation about the arts that more people feel they can be part of." Bunting (2007), p. 19.

Each and every country is entitled to enjoy the fruits of cultural diversity, as well as to have access to the mirror images of its own cultural experiences that will allow it to build a vibrant and responsive society capable of withstanding cultural conflict or exclusion.

Rudder 2006

81

4. Diverse cultural participation – Fostering participation of groups with special needs

According to Elsa Stamatopoulou (2004), participation in cultural life and other cultural rights are important to all people but they are central to people that belong to minorities because of the discrimination and marginalisation that they can all too easily face. So-called minority groups vary from national, cultural and linguistic minorities to immigrants, people with disabilities and those with different religious or sexual preferences.

Children and young people need attention, guidance and opportunities to live meaningful experiences and have healthy emotional experiences that culture can give them. Europe is also facing a demographic change that affects public policy planning in the growing number of elderly people that need tailored services and opportunities. These people vary from the healthy, wealthy and active to those who are socially isolated or living in comparative poverty.

According to the 2004 "Report of a thematic study using transnational comparisons to analyse and identify cultural policies and programmes that contribute to preventing and reducing poverty and social exclusion" by the University of Northumbria for the European Commission, most European countries identified in their actions plans that – as well as the young, elderly or disabled – those that are at the greatest risk of exclusion are vulnerable groups such as immigrants, the unemployed and the homeless.

In 2004 there were approximately 25 million migrants from outside Europe living in European countries. These people were rarely considered part of the political agenda related to participation in cultural life. While civil society organisations often take some responsibility for their inclusion, it is clear that those who do not enjoy the same benefits as the rest of the population are all too easily left out of mainstream cultural life.

Culture and the arts can have an important role in facilitating the participation of these groups in public life. There are many studies on the relationship between culture and the acknowledgement of identity and citizenship, as well as on the socio-economic participation of groups with special needs. Participation in cultural life, art and culture is seen as fundamental to the creation of an inclusive society through an increase in accessibility, strengthened diversity, understanding, sharing and tolerance.

According to the report prepared by the University of Northumbria, in many countries of the European Union there are still too few official policies that connect culture with social cohesion. The report suggested that national policies should acknowledge the role of civil society cultural activities in the prevention of social exclusion. The European Commission's *Joint report on social inclusion* (2001), a summary of policies and initiatives in place or proposed in the member states, concludes that, "in general the [National Action Plans against Poverty and Social Exclusion] do not present coherent plans for fostering the participation of those who are excluded in the creation of culture and cultural activities" and that "when people are prevented from participating fully in economic, social and civil life and/or their access to income and other recourses (personal, family, social and cultural) is so inadequate as to exclude them from enjoying a standard of living and quality of life that is regarded as acceptable by the society in which they live … people often are unable to fully access their fundamental rights."

Fintan O'Toole (2006) reminds us that access and participation are not only physical facts but also related to the images and symbols that a society produces and reproduces. Visibility, representation and body images are part of cultural production. One important aspect – and a threat to the realisation of cultural rights – is that we should not accept or foster all forms of culture. Some applications of culture and tradition can lead people into situations in which their fundamental rights and freedoms are at stake. Protection of vulnerable groups is therefore particularly important – there is a principle of non-discrimination that needs to apply to everyone.

The references to groups of specific needs in this chapter are intended to serve as a sample of existing practices and policies and not to offer a full and exhaustive picture of the situation.

4.1 People with disabilities

The rights of people with disabilities are mentioned in several international instruments, among them the United Nations Convention on the Rights of Persons with Disabilities that came into force, after it's 20th ratification, in May 2008. The convention includes many accessibility issues, including participation in cultural life in Article 30. The convention has been signed by many European states and has been ratified by Croatia, Hungary, Spain (all in 2007) and San Marino (2008). The terms "disability" and "handicap" are also included in the United Nations Standard Rules on the Equalization of Opportunities for People with Disabilities, which were drafted during the Universal Decade for People with Disability (1983-92). The standard rules, however, are not a legally binding treaty.

Article 30 – Participation in cultural life, recreation, leisure and sport

1. States Parties recognize the right of persons with disabilities to take part on an equal basis with others in cultural life, and shall take all appropriate measures to ensure that persons with disabilities:

   a. Enjoy access to cultural materials in accessible formats;

   b. Enjoy access to television programmes, films, theatre and other cultural activities, in accessible formats;

   c. Enjoy access to places for cultural performances or services, such as theatres, museums, cinemas, libraries and tourism services, and, as far as possible, enjoy access to monuments and sites of national cultural importance.

2. States Parties shall take appropriate measures to enable persons with disabilities to have the opportunity to develop and utilize their creative, artistic and intellectual potential, not only for their own benefit, but also for the enrichment of society.

3. States Parties shall take all appropriate steps, in accordance with international law, to ensure that laws protecting intellectual property rights do not constitute an unreasonable or discriminatory barrier to access by persons with disabilities to cultural materials.

4. Persons with disabilities shall be entitled, on an equal basis with others, to recognition and support of their specific cultural and linguistic identity, including sign languages and deaf culture.

5. With a view to enabling persons with disabilities to participate on an equal basis with others in recreational, leisure and sporting activities, States Parties shall take appropriate measures:

   a. To encourage and promote the participation, to the fullest extent possible, of persons with disabilities in mainstream sporting activities at all levels;

   b. To ensure that persons with disabilities have an opportunity to organize, develop and participate in disability-specific sporting and recreational activities and, to this end, encourage the provision, on an equal basis with others, of appropriate instruction, training and resources;

   c. To ensure that persons with disabilities have access to sporting, recreational and tourism venues;

   d. To ensure that children with disabilities have equal access with other children to participation in play, recreation and leisure and sporting activities, including those activities in the school system;

   e. To ensure that persons with disabilities have access to services from those involved in the organization of recreational, tourism, leisure and sporting activities.

United Nations Convention on the Rights of Persons with Disabilities

Former Special Rapporteur on Disability of the United Nations Commission for Social Development, Sheikha Hissa bint Khalifa bin Ahmed al-Thani, stated in a conference in Jordan in 2004 that there is a need to put special focus on women with disabilities and that many children are born disabled and lack the necessary attention to enjoy cultural life. She said that lack of information deepens the gap between people with disabilities and the public at large, and that people with disabilities in many countries are not aware of their right to participate in cultural life. She also underlined that people with disabilities should not only enjoy access to cultural services but also to the means of creation and expression, decision-making processes and communication.[29]

29. Interarts (2004).

The access of disabled people to culture is a democratic responsibility, but in many European countries it is an obligation too. The year 2003 was named as the European Year of People with Disabilities. During the year, the Council of the European Union adopted a resolution on accessibility of cultural infrastructure and cultural activities for people with disabilities (2003/C 134/05). This resolution makes recommendations to the member states in order to improve the physical accessibility of culture. Emphasis is placed on heritage, archaeological and cultural sites and events, as well as on cultural information through new technologies and instruments to facilitate accessibility to cultural and artistic experiences. The resolution is not legally binding but has political importance.

The revised European Social Charter (Council of Europe, 1996) mentions in Article 15 – on the right of persons with disabilities to independence, social integration and participation in the life of the community – that access to cultural activities is a means to promote social integration and participation in the life of the community. The Committee of Ministers of the Council of Europe adopted a recommendation (No. R (92) 6) on a coherent policy for people with disabilities on 9 April 1992. This recommendation includes access to cultural life and leisure and cultural activities.

8. Leisure time and cultural activities

8.1. All leisure, cultural and holiday activities should be made accessible to people with disabilities. In addition, special activities for them should be provided, when requested by people with disabilities, and where the conditions permit them. Active participation of people with disabilities in all cultural, social and political activities should be promoted, including the opportunity for involvement at a professional level.

8.2. Structural, technical, physical and attitudinal obstacles which limit the enjoyment of the above activities should be removed. In particular, access to cinemas, theatres, museums, art galleries, tourist venues and holiday centres should be improved. Access to means of transport and independent mobility should be encouraged. Awareness training for staff working in leisure and cultural centres should be made widely available. Cultural and leisure venues should be planned and equipped so that they are accessible and can be enjoyed by people with disabilities.

8.3. General guide books on leisure, tourism and culture should include all possible information on facilities available to people with disabilities, including transport, hotels, restaurants and sports facilities. They should indicate by accessibility symbols, essential access facilities including toilets, facilities for people with sensory and learning difficulties, availability of assistance, etc. The symbols should follow international conventions, and the keys should be given in several languages. Such guides should be available in accessible forms, including Braille, large print and tape.

8.4. All means to improve access and enjoyment of leisure, culture and tourism for specific groups of people with disabilities should be introduced. Examples may include:

– specific guide books for special categories of people with disabilities, describing particular facilities for people with learning difficulties or who are visually impaired;
– encouragement of the use of audio cassettes providing specific guides for visually impaired people;
– provision of sign interpretation for cultural and leisure activities;
– provision of audio-description in theatres and cinema for visually impaired people;
– flexible arrangements for seating to enable visually and hearing impaired people to have access to suitable places in cultural performances;
– provision of models, maps and relief plans for people with sensory and learning impairment;
– public promotion of an "accessibility chart".

8.5. Government institutions, leisure and cultural organisations should develop comprehensive access policies and action programmes designed to bring significant and lasting improvements in access for all people with disabilities.

As for national constitutions, Romania is one of the few countries that mentions the cultural rights of people with disabilities in its constitution. Article 50 of the Romanian Constitution accords special protection so that access to and participation in community life is fully secured for disabled people. The constitutions of Moldova and Portugal also make provision for the rights of people with disabilities (Articles 51 and 71, respectively), even though the word "culture" is not mentioned specifically.

Texts in France that deal with people with disabilities and culture provide for a wider perspective on offering full citizenship. "Every person has a right to the solidarity of the national collective that guarantees by virtue of this national obligation the access to fundamental rights of all citizens, especially … to education, training and professional orientation, to work, to leisure, to tourism, to culture, to information and to the information technologies and to the full exercise of his/her citizenship."[30] In France the laws of 30 June 1975 and 20 December 1993 guarantee the access of people with disabilities to cultural institutions. The National Commission of Culture and Disability was founded in 2001 by decree. Furthermore, the Law 2005-102 of 11 February 2005 ensures equality of rights and opportunities, participation and citizenship to people with disabilities. In 2006 the ministry of tourism signed a National Culture Tourism Convention that launched a "Tourism and Incapacity" seal for those organisations that fulfilled accessibility criteria.[31] In 2003, the ministry of culture and communication proposed to introduce an exception to authors' rights (in France) to authorise the reproduction of literary works in adapted forms for people with disabilities.[32] In 2006, the ministry established a National Commission on Culture and People with Disabilities that affirms the right of people with disabilities to develop their artistic creativity. French legislation also includes laws on access to museums. In 2007, the ministry published a Charter of Access (*Charte d'accueil*) developed jointly by the national commission, the association ARCHIMED and the Association of People with Disabilities, in a guidebook on accessibility to art and culture. The guidebook has three different parts: on accessibility to buildings, information and community, and access to cultural attractions.[33] The guidebook forms part of a series of publications on culture and accessibility for people with disabilities that the ministry has been publishing since 2004.

The French Ministry of Culture and Communication chose two establishments as pilot "places" to develop the accessibility of people with disabilities to cultural establishments; the City of Sciences and the Quai Branly Museum:
– the City of Sciences; since 1986 it has had a special department in charge of accessibility to exhibitions and services, and it was among the first to receive the "Tourism and Incapacity" seal. It has adopted measures including the use of materials that can be touched, and guided tours in sign language;
– the Quai Branly Museum has taken into account the accessibility of people with disabilities in its design and architecture. The objective was to plan a cultural space accessible to those with disabilities while avoiding segregation from the general public. A number of experts and people with disabilities were consulted on the project in order to produce a series of recommendations that were taken into account in its construction and displays.

30. Speech of the minister for culture in the National Commission of Culture and Disability, 1 June 2006.
31. More information at: www.tourisme.gouv.fr/fr/z2/handicap/label_national/qui_quoi.jsp.
32. The ministry has had difficulties in obtaining authors' rights. Source: Vidal (2007).
33. Available at: www.culture.fr or www.culture-handicap.org.

Some European countries have invested in cultural services for people with disabilities.

Finnish law (638/1992) has established a library for blind people. Changes in the legislation on creators' rights (in force since 1 January 2006) have facilitated access for disabled people: for example, plastic arts that can be touched, translation of books into sign language, versions of popular songs in sign language, among other initiatives. In 2003, the government of Prime Minister Matti Vanhanen underlined in its action plan the cultural rights of children, disabled people and minority groups. The action plan acknowledged Finland as "a society that is based on knowledge, information and creativity. The values of the country are equality, tolerance, internationalisation, responsibility for the environment and the equality between men and women. Cultural rights and the capacity of active citizenship will be promoted through education."[34] The programme acknowledges the role of the country as one of the most developed when it comes to modern technology, multiculturalism and the needs of linguistic groups. The previous government had adopted policies in 2003 to improve access to culture in public art and cultural institutions. The programme underlines the needs of children with special needs, including measures for the accessibility of cultural services in order to fulfil their own cultural activities. Since 2005, the ministry of education and culture has granted subsidies to physical access projects.

In Iceland, the Icelandic Library for the Blind is operated in accordance with Act No. 35/1982 and Regulation No. 201/1987 to ensure access to printed material for the blind. The library's board includes representatives of the Icelandic Association of Blind People, special education teachers, the Library and Information Science Association and the ministry of culture. In Italy, the ministry for cultural heritage and activities signed a decree in December 2007 that provides for new publications to be transferred to digital format for visually impaired people. Under Article 4141 of the Flemish legislation on territory, urbanism and heritage, all new cinema theatres need to be accessible for people with disabilities. In 1998, the Czech Republic published a national plan for the provision of equal opportunities for people with disabilities that includes a provision to facilitate audio recordings for visually impaired people and physical access (mainly wheelchair access) to cultural services.

In 2007, Arts Council England published a study on cultural opportunities for people with disabilities and the socially excluded in response to a call from the Department for Culture, Media and Sport (DCMS). Between 2003 and 2006 the DCMS aimed to increase the proportion of these groups participating in cultural and arts

---

34. Government action plan, 2003.

activities. However, survey results showed no significant change in participation by these groups. The British and Irish sign languages are officially recognised[35] and the Sign Language Partnership Group works closely with local and regional government to improve access to public services. Furthermore, the Museums, Libraries and Archives Council has published a collection of 12 guides on how to reply to the needs of people with disabilities as well as a Disability Equality Scheme for 2007-10 and a Disability Equality Duty.[36] The 12 publications are helpful guides and include issues ranging from physical accessibility to consulting, training and technology. Also, Arts Council England and Arts Council Wales have both published disability equality schemes.

The summary policy paper of the Irish Arts Council from 2005 acknowledges the lack of cultural training opportunities for people with disabilities but also expresses the aim of offering people with disabilities the widest possible access to cultural life and services, as well as funding opportunities for arts activities. The Swedish Government has given a mandate to the Swedish Arts Council to carry out disability policy in the field of culture. The policy includes offering support to cultural institutions all over Sweden in their efforts to improve opportunities available to people with disabilities.

In many countries civil society organisations are strong players in fostering access. Civil society often has a crucial role in assuring rights and satisfactory living conditions for people with disabilities.

In Lithuania, the Open Air Museum of the Centre of Europe organises programmes for disabled people and in Bulgaria several government-supported NGOs work in the field of integrating children with disabilities into public life, including cultural life. In the Flemish Community of Belgium, people with hearing disabilities have been trained as guides in the Royal Museums of Art, and the Comete programme is addressed to people with mental disabilities. At the local level, there are various initiatives. Athens hosted the first Documentary and Disability film festival in 2007 (www.ameamedia.gr/en/festival/festival-09) and in Bulgaria the municipality of Lovech organises an annual conference of painters with disabilities. Other examples around Europe include tailored media programmes and products.

---

35. British Sign Language (BSL) and Irish Sign Language (ISL) were embraced within the Belfast/Good Friday Agreement and in March 2004 the secretary of state in the UK announced the formal recognition of BSL and ISL as languages in their own right following similar recognition of BSL in Great Britain.
36. "45 000 public bodies across Great Britain are covered by the Disability Equality Duty (DED), which came into force in December 2006. The DED is meant to ensure that all public bodies – such as central or local government, schools, health trusts or emergency services – pay 'due regard' to the promotion of equality for disabled people in every area of their work." Source: DED website, www.dotheduty.org.

There are many international organisations that work in the field of securing a dignified life for the disabled and helping them access all forms of public life. These include Inclusion International, United Nations Enable, European Disability Forum, Disabled Peoples' International, Disability Rights Promotion International, Disability World and Child Rights Information Network. Disability Rights Promotion International has two national chapters in Europe, in Croatia and in Sweden. The organisation has worked in Croatia to develop training materials and a monitoring system to address disability discrimination globally.

As well-intended as most of the policy initiatives and programmes in different countries are, international organisations remind us that while tailored approaches and distinctive programmes are needed, it is also important to make people with disabilities feel – without patronising them – that they form part of society. Ensuring physical accessibility of cultural services and equipment is a major step, but at the same time it is important to work closely with people with disabilities in order to produce policies that respond to their special needs and promote social cohesion with the rest of the society. It is clear that much more research and information is needed in order to gain a more accurate picture of their cultural needs and participation levels. There is also the challenge of developing better national systems for securing access and participation of people with disabilities in cultural life.

4.2 Ethnic, national and linguistic minorities

A particular ethnic group may have the right to practice the cultural life of that group but the test of the policy to deliver that right is whether any individual member of that group can enjoy that right freely and equitably.

Sengupta 2002

In the second half of the last century, many European countries attempted to create a cohesive national culture in which minorities could feel at home. This was done through measures that ranged from anti-discrimination to assimilation and from integration to intercultural co-existence. Today, more than ever, the reality of societies is multicultural, intercultural and transcultural – and it is vital that governments design educational, social, cultural and language policies that allow a multiplicity of groups to cohere. In this framework, access and participation and cultural self-realisation hold enormous importance. They can provide an enabling environment for different groups to avoid isolation, cultural ghettoisation and tensions in living together. They also provide people with opportunities and greater individual choice.

Article 27 of the International Covenant on Civil and Political Rights states that people belonging to ethnic, linguistic and religious minorities have the right to "enjoy their own culture, to profess and practice their own religion, or to use their own language". These same rights are acknowledged in the United Nations Declaration on the Rights of Persons Belonging to National or Ethnic, Religious and Linguistic Minorities (1992). Other related instruments with a cultural rights dimension include the Declaration on Race and Racial Prejudice, the United Nations Convention on the Rights of the Child (1989) and the United Nations Convention on the Elimination of All Forms of Racial Discrimination (Article 5 is on the right to equal participation in cultural activities). The recently adopted United Nations Declaration on the Rights of Indigenous Peoples has many references to cultural rights, participation and access in cultural life.

In Europe there are several important international instruments that acknowledge the protection – and participation – of minorities in Europe. The European Charter for Regional or Minority Languages was adopted on 5 November 1992 and has been ratified by 24 Council of Europe member states; Norway, Finland and Hungary being among the first to sign and ratify the convention. Access to and participation in cultural life and the commitments to enable both are mentioned in Article 12 on cultural activities and facilities, as they are considered to be ways to secure linguistic and cultural diversity and access to expression.

The Framework Convention for the Protection of National Minorities of the Council of Europe (1995) has been ratified by 39 member states (as of December 2009). It is an instrument for the protection of national minorities and the rights and freedoms of people belonging to them. Apart from acknowledging the universality of human rights and the rights of people belonging to national minorities – their basic rights, freedoms and linguistic rights – the convention, in Articles 5 and 6, requires states to put into place conditions for promoting and safeguarding national minorities' cultural life and the encouragement of intercultural dialogue.

Article 5

1. The Parties undertake to promote the conditions necessary for persons belonging to national minorities to maintain and develop their culture, and to preserve the essential elements of their identity, namely their religion, language, traditions and cultural heritage.

2. Without prejudice to measures taken in pursuance of their general integration policy, the Parties shall refrain from policies or practices aimed at assimilation of persons belonging to national minorities against their will and shall protect these persons from any action aimed at such assimilation.

Article 6

1. The Parties shall encourage a spirit of tolerance and intercultural dialogue and take effective measures to promote mutual respect and understanding and co-operation among all persons living on their territory, irrespective of those persons' ethnic, cultural, linguistic or religious identity, in particular in the fields of education, culture and the media.

2. The Parties undertake to take appropriate measures to protect persons who may be subject to threats or acts of discrimination, hostility or violence as a result of their ethnic, cultural, linguistic or religious identity.

Article 15

The Parties shall create the conditions necessary for the effective participation of persons belonging to national minorities in cultural, social and economic life and in public affairs, in particular those affecting them.

The political changes in Europe and the fear of ethnic conflicts have led to the formulation of international instruments by the Council of Europe and the Organization for Security and Co-operation in Europe (OSCE), supervised by its High Commissioner on National Minorities. At the moment, only national minorities are currently protected by those instruments, but as Will Kymlinka (2005) has written, "since the actual rights being codified are not based on claims of historic settlement and territorial concentration, there is no reason why they should not be extended to apply to immigrant groups as well. And there is currently a movement within both the Council of Europe and the OSCE to move back to the original Article 27 of the International Covenant on Civil and Political Rights model that attempts to articulate universal cultural rights applicable to all minorities, new or old, large or small, dispersed or concentrated." The European Union requires its member states to take action against ethnic discrimination and racist behaviour. However, the protection of immigrant people and their right to participate in cultural life is still insufficient and there is a need to draft more efficient instruments in this field.

To compare cultural policy programmes for minorities in different countries, Vladimir Bina (2006) suggests a practical division of minorities into three groups: indigenous people, national minorities and migrants – even though there are several countries in Europe that have large ethnic minorities that are not considered separately within national legislation.

Countries have resolved minority issues in different ways and there are a number of exhaustive studies on cultural policy, cultural diversity and the participation of national, ethnic, cultural or linguistic minorities in cultural life. An excellent source is the Compendium of Cultural Policies and Trends in Europe managed by the Council of Europe and ERICarts that displays a large database of good practices in the field of intercultural dialogue. Another recent study also carried out by ERICarts is "Sharing diversity – National approaches to intercultural dialogue in Europe" (2008), which presents a detailed overview of the politics and practices of European Union member countries.

Defining a national or ethnic minority is not always an easy task. The minority rights specialist Asbjørn Eide has even called the word "minority" misleading as, outside Europe, nation states are often composed of a large number of groups, none of which make up a majority.

According to the 2004 "Report of a thematic study using transnational comparisons to analyse and identify cultural polices and programmes that contribute to preventing and reducing poverty and social inclusion" by the University of Northumbria for the European Commission, all the eight countries studied recognised that immigrants and refugees cannot integrate without proper language training. Language has been identified as a major element in access to cultural life and has played a significant role in policies in different countries.

In Finland the concept of a Sami is based almost exclusively on linguistic criteria. A Sami is a person who identifies him or herself as Sami and whose mother tongue is Sami – or at least one of whose parents or grandparents is Sami. In 1995 this definition was enlarged to include other types of descendants as well. The Finnish Constitution (Article 17) guarantees the right of national minorities, the Sami and the Roma people to maintain and develop their culture. The Finnish broadcasting company is obliged by a law (1999) to offer information in Romani. The rights of the Sami people to maintain their cultural autonomy and language are guaranteed in the Finnish Constitution (Article 121). Sami is not an official language, but its position is secured through legislation. The languages that have an official status are Finnish and Swedish.

However, Norway does include Sami as one of its two official languages. The languages considered minority languages are Sami, Kven/Finnish, Rodi and Romani. These groups are also considered as national minorities. In Norway, the basis of the government's policy towards the Sami people is that the State of Norway was originally established on the territories of two peoples, Norwegians and Sami, and both have the right to develop their own culture and language. According to Norway's second periodic report on the implementation of the provisions of the European Charter for Regional or Minority Languages, there are no accurate estimates of the number of inhabitants belonging to national minorities in Norway, since no statistics of ethnic origin are kept. Nonetheless, the official policy towards national minorities is to strengthen their ability to cultivate their own cultures. On 8 December 2000, the Norwegian Government presented a White Paper to parliament (Storting) on national minorities policy. The report includes ways of ensuring equal conditions for participation in society and the preservation of language, culture and cultural identity, and describes official plans for further work in this field. The paper included an apology for the earlier encroachment on cultural minorities. Also between 1998 and 2000, the Norwegian Government ran a programme on art and multicultural society in order to promote multicultural art initiatives within national cultural institutions and the access of minority artists to cultural networks and exchanges.

Since 2000, the Sami language has also been considered as an official minority language in Sweden. Sweden recognises five national minorities – Sami, Finns, Finns who speak Meänkieli, Yiddish speakers and Roma. The recognition is based on their time of settlement in the country, and on their self-identification. These groups are given special provision in some sociocultural fields such as education.

The Sami represent an indigenous nation in Europe but Sami is not by far the only minority or non-state language in Europe. The European Bureau for Lesser-Used Languages, an NGO that promotes languages and linguistic diversity, estimates that today there are approximately 46 million people in the European member states that speak a lesser-used, regional or minoritised language. Another agency working in this field is Eurolang; a specialist news agency that "provides, on a regular basis, relevant and current news about Europe's regional, stateless and minority language communities, to NGOs, the media, European, State and local government, academia, researchers and the general public".

At the end of the European Year of Languages in 2001, the European Parliament adopted a resolution recommending measures to promote linguistic diversity and language learning. Later in February 2002, the European Council adopted a resolution in which it asked the European Commission to submit proposals for actions aimed at promoting linguistic diversity and language learning. The action plan on the promotion of language learning and linguistic diversity adopted by the European Commission in 2003 includes 45 actions (for 2004-06) in three areas: extending the benefits of language learning to all citizens as a lifelong activity; the need to improve the quality of language teaching at all levels; and the need to build in Europe an environment which is favourable to languages.

As of December 2009, 24 countries had ratified the European Charter for Regional or Minority Languages. In countries with national minorities, language classes should be made available if there is a sufficient number of students (the qualifying number depends on each country). However, in some countries, like Italy, minority languages do not enjoy legal recognition as a subject to be taught in schools, even though measures and legislative action have been carried out in order to safeguard the linguistic rights of minorities. The Italian Constitution (Article 6) refers to additional legislation for the protection of linguistic minorities. The cultural rights, mainly linguistic rights, of the seven official (eight, when including the Roma) minorities as well as some linguistic communities are secured in Law 482/1999 – which led to the founding of the National Fund for the Safeguard of Linguistic Minorities. There is no national legislation related to cultural activities of recent immigrant communities; the regional and local levels are more active in this area.

The Bulgarian Constitution ensures that non-Bulgarian speakers have the right to use and study their language alongside the compulsory study of the Bulgarian language. In Bulgaria, an Internet portal was set up to provide information on legal instruments, integration processes and organisation; the target group being institutions and NGOs working in the field of minority issues. Bulgaria has adopted the National Framework Programme on Equal Integration of Roma into Bulgarian Society (1999), which includes cultural issues among its principles. For the implementation of the programme, the active participation of the Roma community is regarded as crucial. The National Plan on the Roma Inclusion Decade (2005-15) aims at integrating Roma people into Bulgarian society. Activities are diverse, from support programmes and projects for cultural and social integration at municipal level to setting up cultural clubs, Internet portals, arts groups, libraries and education courses, among other initiatives. An important element is the improvement of the media and public image of the Roma people.

Under Ukrainian legislation the population belongs either to the Ukrainian majority or to a national minority, which have been accorded basic cultural rights since the Declaration of the Rights of Nationalities of 1991. In Estonia, Article 49 of the constitution states that everybody in Estonia has the right to preserve their ethnic identity. The Estonian legal framework rests on the National Minorities Cultural Autonomy Act (1993), which sets out the cultural rights, linguistic rights, establishes cultural autonomy bodies based on representation, and maintains cultural customs and traditions. In Estonia, the definition of a minority is based on cultural and ethnic characteristics different from the national culture, but also on the wish of cultural minorities to, "collectively maintain their cultural customs, religion or language which are the basis of their common identity".

Article 20 of the Albanian Constitution guarantees the right of ethnic minorities to develop, express and preserve cultural habits and traditions. In Albania, Greeks, Macedonians, Vlachs and Roma have been officially recognised as cultural groups, but as the country is in the process of redefining cultural policies, there are specific questions to address, especially access of minorities to cultural life. The Polish Constitution ensures that national and ethnic minorities enjoy cultural freedoms and linguistic rights. In 2005, Poland adopted the National and Ethnic Minorities and Regional Languages Act, which describes the difference between national and ethnic minorities identified with an existing state and people without a country, though it leaves out new migrants. The biggest ethnic minority, the Roma, receives considerable public funding to foster participation in culture even though their cultural activities are more inclined towards the preservation of Roma cultural traditions than participation of the Roma in Polish national culture.

In the Romanian Constitution, Article 6 acknowledges the rights of those belonging to national minorities to preserve, develop and express their ethnic, cultural, linguistic and religious identity. The revision of the 1991 constitution approved by parliament and adopted by a constitutional referendum in 2003 included the right of national minorities to use their native language in dealing with the governmental administration. Romania has 19 officially recognised ethnic groups. The Romanian Ministry of Culture and Religious Affairs runs several specific programmes that support the participation of minority groups in cultural life, from organising cultural events to measures to support the preservation of cultural heritage.

Austria has six officially recognised national minorities (Slovenes, Croats, Hungarians, Czechs, Slovaks and Roma). According to the report "Cultural diversity in Austria" and the compendium report they are entitled to apply for support for cultural activities, but there are no programmes to foster participation in cultural life further.

In the Netherlands, there is only one officially recognised national minority group, the Frisians. In Denmark, despite a large population of foreign-born Danes or Danes of ethnic origin, the only officially recognised minority is the German-speaking one and there is no legal framework concerning the cultural rights of minorities in the country. There have been, however, some initiatives related to the rights of people with an immigrant background. The Club Theater-2-nights of the Danish Royal Theatre provides considerable discounts to immigrant people with the intention of attracting greater participation in the performing arts.

In Lithuania, no legal or official difference between national minorities and other minorities is made and the legislation recognises the right of a person to choose the minority to which they belong. Lithuania was the first country in central and eastern Europe to pass a Law on National Minorities (1989). This law secures the rights of minorities to receive support for activities for participation in cultural life, access to information and the establishment of cultural organisations. Lithuania has an inter-ministerial Programme of Integration of National Minorities into Society for the years 2005-10, which was approved in 2004. The programme had three main objectives: integration of national minorities into Lithuanian social, cultural and economic life; preservation of the ethnic identity of minorities; and development of coherent relationships among minorities. Since 2000, Lithuania has also had a specific programme for the integration of Roma into Lithuanian society, which includes development of cultural life.

The Slovenian Constitution lists three official minorities (Hungarian, Italian – Article 11 – and Roma), which have their own articles to guarantee social and cultural rights (Articles 64 and 65 – Article 65 acknowledges that the status of the Roma people will be regulated by law but so far no such law has been adopted) even though other minorities have constitutional cultural rights (Article 61). In budgetary terms, the Roma people receive most of the financial support. The compendium report on Slovenia notes: "the Ministry of Culture is the most active of all ministries in attempting to form a special model on the protection of cultural rights of all minorities, which is a result of combining theoretical and practical experience originating from particular issues and their needs. The model is a result of the recognition that an active intervention on the part of the government in complex social situations is necessary in order to facilitate positive intercultural and interethnic relationships. The model also includes constant evaluation and improvements to achieve actual, and not only formal, equity for participation in cultural life." Furthermore, the Exercising of the Public Interest in Culture Act from 2002 acknowledges the special cultural needs of people with disabilities and different minority groups, and sets policy principles that include fostering participation. The municipalities are required by law to respond to the cultural needs of their inhabitants that are identified through local cultural programmes.

The Law on Culture of Azerbaijan recognises the right to cultural identity in Article 8. This article is supported by several other legislative instruments such as International Co-operation in the Cultural Sphere (Article 48), International Exchange in the Cultural Sphere (Article 49) and Co-operation in the Sphere of Conservation of Cultural Values, which aim at securing the connection of minorities with their "historical motherlands". The support for minorities to participate in their culture includes giving support to amateur performances and organisations and the organisation of exhibitions and other activities that make minorities aware of their "cultural values".

Hungary has a large population of national minorities; there are 12 recognised minority groups and one ethnic minority group (the Roma people). Their collective and individual rights are recognised in the Act of National and Ethnic Minorities from 1993. The definition of a minority is based on self-identification by a person belonging to a minority group.

Croatia has 16 official minority groups that all receive support from the state. Cultural activities are mostly aimed at safeguarding cultural traditions. The state support includes not only financing of cultural activities and social cohesion programmes but also a number of libraries that function as reference points for national minorities. In Georgia, even though no specific laws on minorities exist, in principle the cultural rights of minorities are secured in the constitution (the clause on equality) and in the laws on education, culture and broadcasting. These instruments guarantee linguistic rights and the maintenance of culture and development of creative activities.

In Belgium, there is no official definition of minorities. In the Flemish Community there is a minority policy for the period from 2004 to 2010, which aims at building a cohesive and democratic society. Among the goals of the policy, cultural activity should reflect the diversity of the country by 2010, so that members of different minorities can identify with it.

The Swedish Arts Council has been financing the performing arts needs of official national minorities through annual subsidies of SEK 7 million (approximately €772 000) since 2000. Approximately half of this sum is given to Sami and Finnish theatres. During recent years, the council has strengthened the policy on contracts with regard to diversity and gender equality (in the case of the council this means contracting more men!). There is also a minority desk officer, who gives information, and regional diversity advisers who work to increase the accessibility of programmes for all themes related to diversity,

In the United Kingdom, in 1998, Arts Council England published an action plan in favour of cultural diversity that was based on four main strategic goals: diversity, access, development and support. The plan was called Towards a Greater Diversity, and the author, Naseem Khan, recognised that there has been an improvement especially in financial terms. In 2000, statistical information was compiled on the attendance of minorities at cultural events. The results underlined the importance of developing relationships between art institutions and all communities. The Arts Council replied to the demand and included diversity as one of its main principles. The 2003 survey of national statistics showed that minorities in the United Kingdom have a high level of participation in cultural activities and seemingly a greater sensibility towards arts and culture than the rest of the population.

Ireland has no official minorities even though the Roma population has been calling for such recognition. There are, however, measures to deal with the cultural needs of minorities and immigrants. The Immigrant Council has asked the Arts Council to carry out a study on the cultural needs of black and minority ethnic groups in Ireland.

The media and arts support mechanisms of minority, regional and non-state language groups deserve not only their own chapter but a whole study. There is a great richness of initiatives, programmes and projects on fostering cultural participation through regional, minority or non-state languages.

4.3 The ageing and the young

By 2050, Europe will have a high proportion of elderly people. Already 19 out of 20 of the world's "oldest" countries are in Europe – Italy holds top place with over 19% of the population aged over 65. It is also estimated that Bulgaria will lose a third of its population by 2050, Romania 20% and Poland 10%. According to the United Nations' demographic report on Ukraine (March 2006), it has the lowest birth rate in the world. Even though the impact of immigration will be strong in years to come in many European countries, the number of ageing people will rise considerably while the number of young people will decline. Low birth rates mean that the ageing of the population is not a temporary fact but a far-reaching trend, and in most European counties, there will be many active ageing citizens thinking about ways to enrich their lives.

This population will need infrastructure, services and the means to participate in public and cultural life. There is a noticeable lack of appropriate policies in Europe in relation to elderly people and their participation. Older people are often invisible to policy makers and lost among other priorities. Particular attention needs to be given to the situation of women, who tend to live longer but do not always have the lifetime savings to combat loneliness and financial problems. These people will need improvements in their quality of life that enable them to make the most of their own culture.

Adolfo Morrone, a researcher at the Italian National Institute of Statistics, carried out a study on the participation of elderly people in social and cultural life. His findings show that the participation of this group depends largely on their level of education, and that those that participate most are so-called "young elderly", who meet other recently retired people with a lot of free time.[37] These findings are not very different from other countries and they indicate the need to construct new types of policies and invest more strongly in infrastructure and services that respond better to the needs of the elderly.

> Most of the initiatives that help elderly people access culture are in the hands of civil society or cultural institutions. The Malta Drama Centre, for example, carries out a programme together with a private company that brings arts into residences. In Slovenia the Third Age University provides access to culture and education for elderly people. In France, the ministry of culture and communication gives support to a reading programme that in 2004 included almost 350 readings to elderly patients.

In contrast, as regards children (and young people) many policies have been put in place. In international instruments, the right of children to access and participate in cultural life is secured in the UN Convention on the Rights of the Child (1989). Article 31 states:

1. States Parties recognise the right of the child to rest and leisure, to engage in play and recreational activities appropriate to the age of the child and to participate freely in cultural life and the arts.
2. States Parties shall respect and promote the right of the child to participate fully in cultural and artistic life and shall encourage the provision of appropriate and equal opportunities for cultural, artistic, recreational and leisure activity.

International organisations continue to initiate programmes that foster the participation of young people and children, such as the UN's World Programme of Action for Youth to the Year 2000 and Beyond and the European Union's Youth in Action programme.

---

37. Adolfo Morrone, *Entre ancient et nouveau. Les modèles de participation sociale et culturelle des seniors en Italie*, see: www.cairn.info.

The Portuguese Constitution makes several references to the cultural rights of both the young and the ageing. Article 64 covers the creation of economic, social and cultural conditions that secure the protection of children, the young and the old. The constitution also acknowledges the cultural rights of young people, especially those at work (Article 70) and the rights of elderly people to participate in community life and economic, social and cultural measures for personal fulfilment (Article 72). Apart from the Portuguese Constitution, there are no significant references to the ageing European population in standard legal frameworks nor policy statements. For the moment, it seems that European countries are concentrating efforts more on assuring the participation of the young.

The Romanian Constitution mentions the right of young people to participate in cultural life in Article 50. The Hungarian Constitution provides for the protection of young people and their interests as well as education and training (Article 16), as does the Croatian Constitution, which guarantees the state's protection of children and young people and the creation of social, cultural, educational, material and other conditions for the promotion of the right to a decent life (Article 62). The same target group is mentioned in the Moldovan Constitution (Article 50) together with the state's duty to ensure conditions for young people's free participation in cultural life.

In 2003, Jean-François Hersent carried out a study in France on the cultural practices of adolescents, which shows that they use new forms of cultural consumption and access to culture. The study suggests that the adolescents of today have a concept of time that differs from the previous generation – for example, reading is considered too time-consuming. Technological development and the emergence of its new cultural forms bring about new means of participation.

Even though there has been debate in several European countries about the number of hours devoted to arts in the school curriculum, countries tend to aim other cultural participation campaigns, initiatives and programmes at children and young people. Children and young people are considered priority groups even if the policies do not truly answer their needs and demands. The Building a Culture of Participation study, carried out by the United Kingdom's National Children's Bureau and PK Research Consultancy, proposes guidelines to increase participation of children and young people in decision-making processes. In Ukraine, the design and execution of an educational and cultural programme for children and youth was one of the implementation priorities set out in the Law on the Conceptual Framework of Public Policy, 2005-07.

The Interarts study from 2009 on access of young people to culture, commissioned by the Youth Unit of the Education, Audiovisual and Culture Executive Agency of the European Commission offers an overview of the polices, opportunities, cultural offer, legal frameworks, actors at different levels, civil society keyholders and youth culture trends in the 27 member states of the European Union. The study concludes that cultural policies tend to exclude access of young people to culture as it is something related to "leisure" and that cultural policies are stronger in the field of accessing classical forms of art and cultural activities (heritage, plastic arts, etc.) and less so in the emerging fields of contemporary and media-related forms of activity. The study states – based on 27 national reports – that the main obstacles to young people's access to culture are money and time restraints, lack of transportation, social factors, educational level in some countries and geographical differences in others, the attitudes towards young people and of young people themselves, and the cultural offer itself that does not always meet the needs of young people. The study also states:

Policy documents and strategic plans related to young people and culture (including access to culture in some cases) are reported to exist in the following countries:

• The Programme of state support for work with children and youth for NGOs (2007-10) in the Czech Republic focuses on: professional training and education of volunteers working with youth; education of children and youth about healthy lifestyles, development of mobility and international cooperation.

• Estonia has a Youth Work Strategy (2006-13), emphasising the importance of education, employment, health, intercultural learning, participation of young people in decision-making, consideration of interests and needs of young people in all areas of youth policy.

• The Finnish Youth Policy Development Programme 2007-10 requires every municipality to develop a system for hearing young people. Among priority areas are: fostering participation and active citizenship of the young, preventing marginalisation, education, employment, and living conditions.

• The Ministry of Culture of France has a General Programme for Access to Culture – "Transmission des savoirs et democratisation de la culture" (Knowledge transmission and culture democratisation), aiming among other things to make access to museums and monuments free for young people under 25 (as of April 2009).

• The main policy basis for youth affairs in Germany is the Children and Youth Plan, which enshrines cultural education. Other recent federal plans include the National Integration Plan (2007), which regards culture as a vehicle for dialogue and intercultural competences, and the *National Action Plan for a*

Germany Appropriate for Children 2005-2010, with emphasis on youth participation. The Parliament-instated Commission of Inquiry "Culture in Germany" (final report December 2007) dedicated a chapter to surveying the cultural education field with input from the sector, and made a series of key recommendations. The main public actors responsible for policy development are however the 16 autonomous states or *Länder*.

• Ireland has a National Children Strategy (2000-10) entitled "Our Children, Their Voices", emphasising that if children have a voice in matters which affect them, their lives will be better understood and will benefit from evaluation, research and information on their needs and rights and effectiveness of services.

• In Latvia, the Culture and Creativity Industry Development Programme (2009-13) ensures cross-sector co-operation in the establishment of a "culture school bag", i.e. defining a certain minimum of cultural services which need to be ensured for each child and young person. Another milestone is the State Youth Policy Programme (2005-09) and the Youth Policy Guidelines for 2009-18.

• The Programme of Cultural Education of Children and Youth, initiated by the ministry of culture, ministry of science and education and department of youth affairs in Lithuania (2006-11) aims at stimulating innovative methods of teaching and learning in culture, as well as encouraging public organisations and NGOs to develop cultural education for children and youth. Attention is paid to rural areas.

• The Youth and Family Programme in the Netherlands (since 2007) focuses on: social inclusion, cultural diversity, cultural citizenship, cultural education and participation.

• The Youth Policy Action Plan of Slovakia (2008-09) emphasises cultural activities for children and youth from minority groups, support for interactive and creative events at cultural venues, inter-connections between culture and education, and creation of specific instruments to bring culture and arts closer to children and youth.

• The latest major youth strategy launched by the central government in Spain is the *Interministerial Youth Plan 2005-2008*, which has not been replaced as of May 2009. One of the six major areas contained in the plan refers to "Leisure, Culture and Free Time".

• The Fact Sheet of the Swedish Government's Youth Policy was released on 11 September 2009 and it declares the main goals of youth policy in Sweden to be: to give young people genuine access to influence and welfare, to involve them in international cooperation and to increase their participation.

The government priorities of the work of the ministry of culture include the right of children and young people to culture.[38]

• The UK has several important policy documents related to youth and access to culture, among them: Children's Plan (2007); Developing Accessible Play Space (2003); Strategy Healthy Eating, Healthy Lives (2008); Aiming High for Young People: A Ten-Year Strategy for Positive Activities (2007).

• The Romanian Youth Programme is based on a Policy for Sustaining the Young Generation (2005-08), aiming at increasing the autonomy of young entrepreneurs and businesses in rural areas, involving youth in public life, support for young people's mobility, continuing education and professional training

• The Icelandic Children's Cultural Fund was established in 1994 and is funded mainly by the ministry of culture. The fund aims at supporting artistic and cultural projects specifically designed for children with their active participation. The administrative committee is composed of representatives of artists, teachers and the ministry of culture, among others. Iceland also runs a project called Music for All addressed to school pupils to introduce them to various forms of music. Similar schemes exist in several other countries in northern Europe. This project is a joint venture between local and national authorities.

• Denmark has also fostered active participation by children in culture in various forms from film and music schools to theatre. In 2003, various key institutions established a Network for Children's Culture to serve that purpose and to secure future initiatives for children. In 2006, the network published a plan of action and a report on *Children's culture for all of Denmark.*

• The French Community of Belgium organised a series of training seminars in 1995 and 1996 on culture and children in hospitals, which were later gathered into a publication.[39] As a result, the network Channel-Health was created with the objective of developing health and culture crossover benefits and of creating bridges between artists and hospitals.[40]

Most countries have signed up to Euro<26 Youth Card campaigns. The youth card is an initiative of the European Youth Card Association to promote mobility, access to information and participation. The benefits include services, discounts and other advantages.

---

38. "Culture is essential for the development of children and young people. Knowledge of one's own culture is also a prerequisite for understanding and appreciating the circumstances and values of others." Source: "Time for Culture. The Ministry of Culture at Work", Sweden 2009.
39. www.cultureetdemocratie.be/fr/documents/lart_humanise.doc. Accessed in December 2009.
40. www.cocof.irisnet.be/site/fr/reseauxsante/canalsante/. Accessed in December 2009.

The law related to the fight against discrimination in France states in Article 142 that there is a need to encourage the access of schoolchildren to cultural activities during their free time as well as to sport, new technologies and communication, without the family's resources being a discriminatory factor among students.

4.4 Other groups

Other groups can also find themselves vulnerable or at a disadvantage in relation to participation in cultural life. Those that may need special attention can be people in institutions (prisons, hospitals, mental institutions), those in danger of social exclusion (the homeless, unemployed, people on low incomes), immigrants, and sexual minorities. Several countries support policies concerning access and participation for socially excluded people. Even if the experiences that result tend to be quite local, their impact can be a very positive one.

One example of such an initiative is the French Community of Belgium's Words Without Walls network for arts in prisons, which creates a meeting point between the cultural field, prisoners and civil society. A 1990 agreement between the French ministries of culture and communication, and justice also takes cultural activities into prisons.

There seems to be a significant difference between urban and rural communities as regards participation in cultural life, often due to lower incomes in rural areas and greater difficulties in maintaining cultural services in areas where the population is isolated or sparse.

In Denmark the countrywide programmes strategy (*Kultur i hele landet*, www.kum.dk/sw40238.asp) aims at supporting culture as a cohesive element in the local environment outside the metropolitan area. The 2004 study of the cultural demands of Lithuanian people called for more cultural services accessible for those living in rural areas. Another example of initiatives in rural areas can be found in Scotland.

Sometimes collaboration between sectors is needed to improve access to cultural life, for example in the case of people with poor health.

As a result of a colloquium on culture and health organised in Brussels in 2004, including a workshop on the humanising effects of the arts, the participants set up of a network on Art and Health. This network receives funding from Belgium's French Community and the network Channel-Health. In 2007, the network published a guidebook for health personnel, cultural workers and policy makers.[41] Since 1995 the French Ministry of Culture and Communication has issued guidance on culture in hospitals. The ministries of culture and communication, and health signed an agreement in 1999 to encourage cultural work, including cultural policies for hospitals, different services and co-operation between hospitals and cultural infrastructure.

Family units are too often found to be excluded from active participation. However, some agencies have developed initiatives directed at families.

Arts Council England has developed a Family Friendly Tool Kit to support arts organisations to facilitate the participation of families. The tool kit presents four areas for attention. These include access and facilities (parking, signs, family catering, baby changing, etc.); programming (family-friendly timing, diversity of events and activities, opportunities for hands-on activities, etc.); marketing and communications (family tickets and deals, useful transport links, family strategies, etc.); and customer care (child protection policy, listening to children, awareness training of staff, etc.). The tool kit encourages organisations to develop a family-friendly action plan.

Most countries do not have specific programmes to increase the participation of women in cultural life. There are, though, initiatives for women from minorities to help them to achieve key positions in public institutions. For example, in Bulgaria, the Open Society Institution runs a gender programme and in the Netherlands the ministry of culture and the ministry of social affairs supported research projects on women in the arts and cultural professions.

---

41. Available at: www.cultureetdemocratie.be/fr/documents/ArtetSantepublication.pdf.

5. European experiences – Participation in cultural life

Most European countries have already developed ways of encouraging access to culture and strengthening the participation of citizens in cultural life. This chapter looks at some examples from the European arena of how policy principles are translated into programmes and action. The examples presented vary from participatory processes to facilitating the access of children to cultural experiences. They are not intended to be exhaustive, but to reflect a diversity of approaches.

Access to local cultural heritage: MUSEUM ONLINE (Austria)

(Part of the text is a direct extract from the MUSEUM ONLINE web page: www.museumonline.at/international/en.)

MUSEUM ONLINE is a programme commissioned by the Austrian Ministry of Education, Arts and Culture, and managed by KulturKontakt Austria. The main components of the process are access to art and culture, a participatory approach, and the technical and cultural use of communication – and information technology and education. The main participants are 10-19-year-old students, who acquire different skills through the process and learn about their common heritage. The project aims at the active involvement of the students themselves with the subjects and with the cultural institution functioning as their project partner.

The idea behind MUSEUM ONLINE is to promote co-operation between museums and schools by the use of innovative technology. The application of new communications and information technology represents a substantial component of the project.

Since 1995 more than 450 schools across the whole of Austria – linked with their partner schools as well as numerous museums, arts and cultural institutions from home and abroad – have participated in MUSEUM ONLINE.

Some 14 years after its foundation, MUSEUM ONLINE has already successfully established itself as an active platform that enables museums and schools to enter into contact with each other and at the same time maintain a youth perspective on cultural heritage.

MUSEUM ONLINE should not only appeal to information technology teachers but also – bearing in mind its emphasis on cultural and artistic content – to teachers of fine arts. MUSEUM ONLINE aims at motivating these teachers to benefit from the possibilities offered by multimedia, which prepare the ground for the merging of content, techniques and aesthetics; it should also encourage teachers to explore experimental, new and modern approaches to conveying cultural heritage.

Haptic and Virtual World

The students attending the secondary school in Golling in Lower Austria documented a range of so-called "minor monuments" of their home village; among these are chapels, wells, facade and gable figures, sculptures, street monuments, memorial stones and commemorative plaques and gates. Moreover, they also engaged in the renovation of small chapels under the direction of experts. This blend of the haptic and virtual worlds is characteristic of many projects of MUSEUM ONLINE. Young "media enthusiasts" are particularly successful in achieving a synthesis of computer-technical possibilities and traditional-creative modes of expression at those points where their own life situations can flow into the project. For instance, the virtual galleries that were successfully created by the SPZ Unterweissenbach in order to promote their computer-generated works: the severely handicapped children orient themselves by copying and isolating the paintings of the "great masters" according to their perception of the paintings and their models (the great masters). Another example would be that of young people in search of answers to the following question: "What do museums offer to young people?" One possible solution is provided by the Culture4youth Club, set up in co-operation with the Joanneum Museum on the initiative of the students of the BHAK (school for trade and commerce), Grazbachgasse.

A different approach to the question would be the one adopted by the HBLA (school for commerce and tourism), Ursprung: the school turns into a branch office of the museum. In co-operation with the "House of Nature", the HBLA carried out research on a project about genetic engineering and used the scientific data for the development of computer games.

Participation in cultural life: a resource in the fight against social exclusion (Belgium)

In 1992 the Federal Government of Belgium proposed a "new contract with the citizen" with the intention of building a "society with solidarity".[42] Within this framework the ministry of social integration organised a research and consultation exercise on poverty in Belgium. The target group was composed of people living in poverty, etc. They were invited to collaborate in expressive processes related to mobility and dialogue. The federal government chose two organisations: the Movement ATD Quart Monde and the Public Centre of Social Action (CPAS) section of the Union of Cities and Municipalities in Belgium. The organisations gathered and organised testimonies, surveys, life experiences, good practices, and analyses of social situations and processes of exclusion, poverty and participation in society. Two years of dialogue between organisations, workers, representatives of public authorities, social workers, associations, people on low incomes, teachers and doctors resulted in the report. It was originally based on a double concept: the involvement of people on low incomes in the process and close attention to participation in cultural life. The approach to the theme and the method used by the King Baudouin Foundation were innovative in that they proposed to listen, for the first time, to people on low incomes reflecting on their lives. These project collaborators were active at all stages: from preliminary dialogue to drafting, revision and publication of the report.

The report is divided into four parts: "Family, conditions for existence and health", "Employment and social protection", "Housing and environment" and "Knowledge and culture, learning". Chapter 4.1, "The right to participation, contribution and the construction of culture", includes the following observations: culture is defined from a wide perspective that includes expressions of values, ideas and thoughts as well as cultural heritage, arts and artistic expressions; culture forms part of the fundamental human rights of the individual; making your voice heard is also a fundamental right that can be made real through participation in culture; and culture is closely related to democracy – it is in fact a motor for democracy. Throughout the process it was affirmed that culture is already a central element in social exclusion

---

42. "The right to culture, ten years after the report on poverty", Office of the Fight against Poverty, Precariousness and Social Exclusion".

because cultural barriers, ignorance and uncertainty cause obstacles to political and social participation and affect core values such as family, religion, the process of association and education.[43]

The report identified a series of obstacles to participation in cultural life and underlined recommendations and proposals for public authorities and government. Some of the obstacles included low incomes, financial dependency and the price of cultural events on offer. The proposals included taking into account the right to culture as a fundamental necessity in the minimex indicators[44] (with the eventual intention to establish a cultural minimex) and the development of cultural initiatives that guarantee people on low incomes the opportunity to develop their expressive needs. A strong emphasis was placed on neighbourhood activities in the design and management of the cultural content. The report underlined the assumption that participation in cultural life is a resource in the fight against exclusion. The recommendations and proposals were addressed to victims of poverty as well as to citizens and policy makers in order that they might change the context that generates poverty.

In 2002-03, ten years after the publication of the report, the ministry of integration asked the organisation Kunst en Democratie (www.cultureetdemocratie.be) to evaluate the impact and implications of the report. The organisation's report shows the changes and action taken since the initial publication. The findings show that the Belgian Government has indeed launched "integrative" groups to facilitate the participation of people on low incomes in cultural life. Furthermore, public social service centres receive financial support to promote the cultural and social development of their clients. The report also shows several examples of good practice in projects that connect cultural and social services.

> "Article 27" is an initiative of cultural democratisation and awareness raising, where financial access to cultural services is accompanied by an introduction to culture, including "cultural ambassadors".
>
> www.article27.be/article27/index.php

---

43. "Rapport général sur la pauvreté". Available at www.mouvement-lst.org/documents/1995_rapport_general_pauvrete.pdf.
44. Minimex was a system of social financial support that Belgian Law 07/07/1074 established for marginalised people who receive support from public centres of social action. In 2002, minimex was replaced by a guaranteed minimum income.

Culture for all is a programme of exchange, training and information between cultural operators and associations to facilitate access and cultural practice for the public.

www.cera.be/cera/fr/projects/national

Centres for Expression and Creativity (CECs) were created in the 1980s with the objective of securing the right to culture of people on low incomes. CECs organise creativity workshops in neighbourhoods and in other institutions (hospitals, schools, prisons, etc.). A decree is under preparation to recognise, finance and evaluate the work of the CECs.

www.mouvement-lst.org/documents/2007-05-15_cec_pauvrete_decret_demandes.pdf

The report makes recommendations to:

- equip the cultural sector with physical, financial and other resources to be able to deal with different sections of the public;
- encourage meetings between cultural workers and the social sector;
- propose solutions for mobility and accessibility (decentralisation of cultural activities, public transportation systems);
- strengthen information and make it more understandable for the public;
- find ways for the different levels of government to share common policy goals;
- foster networks and co-operation projects;
- carry out evaluations of existing regulatory frameworks and initiatives;
- reform legislation relating to access to culture;
- increase training;
- incorporate cultural aspects in social training;
- train professionals to connect different agents and sectors;
- carry out awareness-raising campaigns for the general public in collaboration with the media.

The proposals also included a section dedicated to local policies for collaboration between cultural bodies at the local level. The latter were recommended to:

- form local cultural organisations for the citizen;
- increase the participation of people on low incomes in cultural organisations and institutions;
- reorganise local cultural programmes according to the needs of the inhabitants and stimulate local government to integrate participation in culture for all (especially people on low incomes) into strategic planning and the political agenda.

Cultural rights, standards and entitlements (Scotland)

In 2004 the Scottish Executive established a Cultural Commission to map out the state of cultural life in Scotland and to consider what role cultural rights could have to facilitate access to cultural life. In the process, the commission carried out wide-ranging consultations with representatives of the cultural sector. The final report, "Our next major enterprise" published in 2005, presents an exhaustive analysis of the relationship between cultural rights and Scottish cultural life and its infrastructure. According to its findings, the right to participate in cultural life should be protected, including participation in cultural policy planning. The commission established a working group to define a methodical approach to rights, standards and entitlements for different components of the cultural sector. It distinguished between permissive rights and rights of provision. A permissive right is a right permitting cultural freedom and cultural expression, and a right of provision is a right that requires a provision from the state.

The basic structure is the following:
rights ⇨ policies ⇨ standards ⇨ entitlements (specific rights);

which would be the responsibility of:
the minister (Scottish Parliament) ⇨ Scottish Executive ⇨ sectors ⇨ local partnerships (associations/local co-operation).

The recommendations of the Cultural Commission include proposals to:
- recognise and incorporate in the legislation existing rights at European level and in the UK;
- establish four main cultural rights, prepared by the Government of Scotland:
  - to fulfil creative potential;
  - to take part in cultural life;
  - to enjoy an enriching communal life in a satisfying environment;
  - to participate in the design and implementation of cultural policy.

These rights would be considered permissive rights and they should be revised periodically:
- to use the national standards as examples for the preparation of local standards that should be revised every five years;
- to incorporate entitlements in local strategic cultural planning.

The Scottish Executive responded that cultural rights and entitlements can have an impact on the life of the citizen and the communities around Scotland. The executive presented three key responsibilities that guide investments in cultural provision, one of them being access to performing arts throughout Scotland. In December 2006, the Scottish Executive presented a Draft Culture (Scotland) Bill, which was presented to the parliament in early 2008 (now passed and in the process of implementation) after it had been open for consultation by Scottish citizens and cultural institutions to secure, in the words of the Scottish Minister of Culture, Patricia Ferguson, "the largest possible participation in cultural life that brings real benefits to all communities and individuals, and releases their creative potential". The central proposals of the bill included the idea that cultural entitlements should be secured by local administrations after they have consulted the local population on the cultural activities they wish to engage in. The bill also controversially set up a new administrative body, Creative Scotland.

As a part of the process the Scottish Executive worked with representatives of local administration, cultural agencies and others in order to define the development of local cultural entitlements. The collaboration between the executive and local agents also included information on cultural planning, including execution and monitoring of policy. Together with the Culture Bill, the executive published guidelines on the responsibilities of local authorities. The objective was not only to guide the local administrations but also to give support to a number of pathfinder projects in order to investigate and show how cultural entitlements and planning can be successful in putting more people in contact with cultural opportunities. The main principles of the guidelines are related to cultural planning, the nature of cultural entitlements and monitoring. They include a requirement for local authorities to report to the executive on a quality assurance framework for cultural entitlements. The cultural entitlements are to be designed and developed together with the local population. The guidelines include a framework for the development of local cultural entitlements as well as a list of examples of what could be specific rights.

Generic examples of entitlements (specific entitlements might be targeted at particular sections of the community, or community-wide, if appropriate):

The arts
– Introduction to playing musical instruments
– Access to activities involving, e.g. visual arts, craft, dance, drama, etc.

- Diversionary activities in evenings and at weekends (e.g. popular music workshops) designed to attract young people in communities with few recreational options
- Chance to take part in a public art project
- Availability of arts activity referrals for general practitioners, through link up with the NHS and local practices
- Arts activities catering for Gaelic communities/speakers (and other indigenous languages)
- Free or subsidised access to a live performance
- Access to film and media development opportunities
- Chance to plan and participate in community festivals
- Provision of cultural "hubs" in rural or otherwise peripheral communities – with performance, and/or workshop and exhibition space
- Access to multicultural events and activities for all communities, including minority communities, migrant workers or asylum seekers
- Activities for young people who are looked after and accommodated
- Heritage resources (including museums, galleries, archives, ancient monuments)
- Access to local heritage sites
- Reminiscence projects with older people
- Archaeology activities at local sites or museums
- Opportunity to explore and learn about the history of your area using your museum, library and archives
- Access to guided gallery tours, talks or activities
- Access to cultural volunteering opportunities
- Opportunities for local people to interpret museum collections
- Virtual reality tours of sites for people with limited mobility
- Chance to take part in a local project that explores community heritage

Library services
- Free access to books and Internet
- Access to reader development activity
- Access to "homebound" services
- Access to writers' workshops
- Community learning and literacy classes
- Computer and Internet access skills courses

- Mobile library services, with peripatetic reader development and other services for rural communities and those with related needs
- Development of GP referral schemes with libraries (bibliotherapy)
- Opportunities to explore family history
- Early learning opportunities
- Access to information in languages appropriate to community profile

The document includes a section on the contribution of local cultural entitlements to the objectives of local authorities. Some examples include:

Improving health and well-being	– access to dance and drama activities – reminiscence projects with older people – access to library "homebound" services – cultural activities targeted at vulnerable young people who are looked after and accommodated
Building more attractive communities	– community activities for older people, including people in residential care – participation in a public art project – community heritage projects – access to information about local history – multicultural activities
Reducing anti-social behaviour	– diversionary activities for young people in the evening and at weekends in "hot spots" through detached youth and arts workers – using cultural activities to explore inter-generational issues – using cultural activities to explore sectarian issues
Increasing employment prospects	– adult literacy schemes in libraries – apprenticeships for young people and placements in creative industries – training in craft activities or the visual arts – computer and Internet access skills courses in libraries
Engaging young people	– access to film and media development workshops – development of incentivised cards to access cultural facilities – access to music workshops – opportunities to showcase local bands – community history projects exploring themes relevant to young people, e.g. contemporary collections in museums – opportunities to participate in the design of cultural services

Culture for all – Accessibility of art and culture (Finland)

The opportunities for special needs groups to participate in cultural life, and the action taken by the administration to facilitate access, were subjects of a "Culture for all" study (2002). The project was carried out by the Accessibility Committee (2001-02) composed of representatives of disabled people, cultural institutions and external experts, invited by the ministry of education and culture. The committee published its proposals for an action programme in 2004:

> The report paints a vision of an ideal society where all people have equal opportunities to enjoy arts and culture and to express their own creativity. In the vision, art and cultural services are accessible to different publics both physically and in terms of content. In this society, cultural service providers are aware of the different ways in which art consumers move, act, use their senses and process information, and arrange their services accordingly.[45]

In 2004 the proposals were translated into an action programme through practical and theoretical guidelines compiled to help arts and cultural institutions make their services more accessible. Also in 2004, the website Culture for All[46] was launched. The website is primarily addressed to professionals in the field of culture and contains practical information on how to improve accessibility.

Following up on the success of the first phase of the programme, the ministry of education decided to set up an action plan to improve overall cultural access "with special emphasis on safeguarding the cultural rights of cultural minorities and people with disabilities". The action plan was set up for four years (2006-10) under the title Access to Art and Culture for All. As expressed in the outline, "the programme contains measures which the ministry will implement by 2010. Some of the measures can be financed from the reallocation of existing appropriations, while others require an increase in resources from the 2005 level."

45. Minister for Culture Tanja Karpela.
46. www.kulttuuriakaikille.fi/en.php.

According to the website the programme works through:

- information-based guidance;
- resource allocation;
- performance management and monitoring progress in accessibility;
- accessibility expertise in recruitment;
- training of culture professionals;
- equal access to arts and cultural institutions.

Other actions involve making "gradual increments in resources earmarked for supporting cultural activities provided by disability organisations, promoting access to culture, enhancing multiculturalism, combating racism, and supporting the indigenous Sami culture. In addition, the ministry grants discretionary subsidies to sign language theatre and for the publication of easy-to-read literature." There will also be a new advisory board on accessibility issues. The ministry will run an impact evaluation of the programme in 2011 as a starting point for further action.

Participatory arts (Ireland)

Participatory arts is an arts practice that aims at including the public in the process of making and interpreting of art. This idea, first practised by community artists and organisations, is slowly making its way into policy planning as well, especially in the British Isles. Participatory arts is based "on the right of people to contribute to and participate fully in culture; the right to have a voice and the right to give voice" (Fitzgerald 2004) – reflecting international moves to introduce inclusive and participatory art practices. As was said in the Arts Council of Ireland's 2005 discussion paper "participatory arts have their own values. They enable people to make or shape 'their own' art and validate peoples' own artistic perceptions. They equally esteem all genres and value cultural diversity. Participatory arts are inclusive. They give us a more inclusive definition of 'the artist'. They deal with access, ownership, diversity and inclusiveness." Suzana Milevska calls this process "shifting from objects to subjects" and art market researcher Alan Brown categorises participatory arts into five groups:

- inventive arts participation engages the mind, body and spirit in an act of artistic creation that is unique and idiosyncratic, regardless of skill level;
- interpretive arts participation is a creative act of self-expression that brings alive and adds value to pre-existing works of art, either individually or collaboratively;
- curatorial arts participation is the creative act of purposefully selecting, organising and collecting art to the satisfaction of one's own artistic sensibility;
- observational arts participation encompasses arts experiences that you select or consent to, motivated by some expectation of value;
- ambient arts participation involves experiencing art, consciously or unconsciously, that you did not select.

There are several "participatory arts" dialogues in Europe. In 2002, City Arts of Dublin, a community arts centre, produced a civil arts inquiry into the role of arts and culture in civil society, and in 2004 into its function and purpose. The Arts Council of Ireland has participatory arts as one of its 23 policy areas mentioned in the Partnership for the Arts, an action plan for 2006-08: "The Arts Council understands participatory arts to include a broad range of practice where people collaborate with skilled artists to make or interpret art. The core purpose of this work is to develop creative individuals and communities and this is central to the Arts Council's purpose in all art forms, schemes and programmes." The 2005 discussion paper recognises, however, that "there is growing consensus that developing participatory arts needs time, with long-term, multi-agency partnership funds and supports. Good partnerships and sustainable processes take time to develop, to ensure support and expectation for an excellent artistic process on all sides." The council acknowledges the lack of data and statistics on participatory arts and calls for effective mapping exercises.

In order to achieve the goals set for greater arts participation, the council plans to carry out information exchange, networking, training and mentoring of professionals, partnerships and funding opportunities for arts organisations in order to develop best practice standards in participatory arts as part of their artistic programmes. Between 2006 and 2008 the council resolved to work along three different lines of action to ensure a wide take-up in participatory arts support. These involved new funding programmes (for artists working in projects on participatory arts; mentors, trainers and educators; resource organisations, etc.), advocacy, and initiatives to support participatory arts. The Arts Council website lists the aims as to:

- develop appropriate funding criteria and programmes to enable the Arts Council to respond to this evolving area of arts practice;
- establish a new programme directed at supporting participatory arts through sustainable multi-agency partnerships, taking account of the need for adequate resources for artists and key workers; evaluation and critical reflection; pre-project research and development; local, national and international linkages and process-based collaborative work;
- ensure that information on professional development opportunities for artists working in this area is made available;
- facilitate networks that offer support and information-exchange for artists and organisations;
- create a support programme, with others where appropriate, to encourage research, evaluation, organisational development and leadership development directed at enhancing participatory arts practice;
- examine models which will assist in supporting this work on an sustained basis.

The Arts Council website lists publications on various issues from inter-sectorial co-operation (culture and health) to notes on participatory arts. There are also several other sites that offer information on community and participatory arts initiatives. More information can be found through Irish participatory arts networks, civil society and art organisations.

New Territories for Art programme (France)

There are several examples of synergy between official cultural policies and civil society movements. The French programme New Territories for Art (NTA) makes reference to the emergence of creative resources and spaces developed by civil society in parallel to the official art networks. There are several similar experiences in Europe, and the concept of "new territories" does not exclusively refer to the example presented, but is often used to describe new forms, methods and technology in artistic expression.

In France, NTA groups are composed of creative professionals or artists that carry out the management of these open spaces for contemporary creation. The NTA groups are situated in old abandoned industrial areas and aim at contributing to local development. In 2000, the French Ministry of Culture and

Communication commissioned a study to analyse these artistic experiences. To respond to the recommendations of the report "A new era for cultural action", an inter-ministry team was constituted and later incorporated into the Institute of Cities (a public institution that brings together ministries and associations to discuss city-related matters, including arts). The multidisciplinary team gives support to projects, decentralised local administration and services in cultural decentralisation policy.

The ministry of culture and communication and the Institute of Cities signed a multi-annual agreement to facilitate access by the public to culture and to enable social cohesion. The ministry established a national working group on "cultural and arts spaces in the urban environment" in order to gain better knowledge of the processes through which art, the social dimension and the urban environment meet. In the same framework, the regional cultural offices organised a series of meetings. In 2005, a national Conference on New Artistic and Cultural Spaces in the Urban Environment was organised to connect local cultural administrators and creative professionals. Also in 2005, two books were published: one with contributions from more than 80 NTA practitioners in 20 countries: artists, intellectuals, architects and policy makers ("New territories for art", 2005), and one on the impact of these policies on spaces.

General Forum of Culture (the French Community of Belgium)

In 2004, the Minister for Culture and Audiovisual Services of the French Community of Belgium, Favila Laanan, organised a forum called "Etats Généraux de la Culture" (EGC) – the States General of Culture[47] – with the intention to start a "global and coherent discussion of the public intervention in the cultural sector" through consultation of all parts of the cultural field. Its main mission was to guarantee cultural diversity and accessibility. From December 2004 until June 2005, the process invited all cultural practitioners, artists, journalists, academics and cultural or social trainers, the general public, and cultural administrative personnel in the French Community to express their ideas, proposals and expectations. Their opinions were incorporated into a list of "culture priorities" and, after debate in parliament, the

---

47. www.forumculture.be/home.php.

Government of the French Community adopted a resolution on 7 November 2005, which has since served as the basis for cultural policy. On 19 January 2007, the minister presented the first annual evaluation of the follow-up of the forum.[48] It reported on:

– launching culture and sport funds;
– fostering initiatives between the culture sector and schools;
– making museums free to all on Sundays and free throughout the year to school groups and youth associations;
– adoption of a "code of respect" for cultural users;
– enhancing measures relating to reading activities.

Chapter 5 of the document is focused on accessibility and participation. The main findings were that:

– the involvement of the public and recognition of their rights has declined (professionals and cultural "mediators" in all organisations that receive public subsidises need to be trained to recognise rights);
– there is a need to establish stronger links between culture and education (with new regulations to foster artistic expression in schools, an inventory of existing available education services in cultural institutions, and an increasing presence of artists in schools);
– it is important to give support to the connection between local television stations and people and to make local news from other parts of the community accessible;
– there is a need to make museums more attractive (entrance to museums has been free – but only once a month – since 2006, though there is free entrance for children and students all year round);
– the role of libraries needs to be valued more highly and their physical access to public spaces needs to be improved;
– it is important to take action for young people – regulating for youth organisations to reflect the diversity of participation and support individual development; reforming the Youth Council of the French Community to reflect the needs of the users better; disseminating information on arts and cultural activities in schools;
– creation of a web portal in 2006 to facilitate access to cultural information.

123

48. Between November 2005 and December 2006, 80% of the recommended actions were carried out (such as the refinancing of the cultural sector) or are in process of being so (new regulations for the programmes). More information at: www.forumculture.be/home.php.

Access to one's own culture – Sami culture for the Sami (Norway)

Access to one's own culture is one of the basic cultural rights, and several European countries have established mechanisms so that minority cultures within national boundaries can have access to their own cultural traditions and above all to their living language. According to Norway's second periodical report on the implementation of the provisions of the European Charter for Regional or Minority Languages (2002), the Norwegian Ministry of Cultural Affairs has implemented a number of measures to support minority languages as "an overall effort to acknowledge these languages as an expression of cultural wealth". The ministry has acknowledged the importance of fostering cultural activities and facilities for people belonging to minorities, especially the Sami people, through action to support their participation in cultural life.

For many years the efforts to promote the Sami culture concentrated on education and on the preservation and promotion of culture and literature. In recent years, however, the attention has switched to supporting the access of the Sami people to their culture. Action includes setting up a virtual school of the Sami language,[49] a Sami library,[50] museum resources that are also accessible through the Internet,[51] online newspapers, access to festivals and youth activities.

Culture in working life (Sweden)[52]

Help for people to enjoy cultural experiences and access to cultural services is not only aimed at minorities and those in vulnerable groups. As some of the studies have shown, participation in art and culture is in the end taken up by relatively few and there is a large part of the population that take part only occasionally, if ever. This might be due to lack of interest but at times it is the result of the incompatibility of work life with family and leisure time or lack of accessible opportunities. Therefore workplaces can play a great role in promoting access to cultural activities.

---

49. See: www.e-skuvla.no/?index=Info.
50. See: http://troms.kulturnett.no/bibliotek/samisk/default_nor.htm.
51. See: www.samimuseums.no.
52. Parts of the text in this chapter have been provided by Ingrid Hemström from Kulturradet.

The Culture in Working Life fund was established in the mid-1980s as a direct result of earlier research and development work by the Swedish Arts Council (*Kulturradet*). Its aim is to advance cultural democracy by involving people in artistic or cultural activities without the requirement of previous experience. The Swedish Parliament established the fund in 1974 to incorporate cultural policy as part of the general welfare programme. This opened the use of state investment to promote culture in working life. Ingrid Hemström (2008) wrote as a response to an email requesting information on this initiative, "much responsibility was given to organisations such as the Swedish Trades Union Congress (LO) and the Swedish Confederation of Professional Employees (TCO), which were seen as having greater possibilities than cultural institutions for reaching culturally deprived groups within society. Funding for the project 'Culture in Working Life' has varied from around SEK 1 million to SEK 7.5 million per year from 1985 to 2007. The project is active within the entire cultural sphere, often in collaboration with regional or local authorities."

The project aims at having a long-term effect and to serve as an example for other similar initiatives. From 2008, aid has been given only on condition that at least 50% of project costs are financed by other means, a rise of 25% on previous years.

Between 1997 and 2007, some 540 projects were awarded grants. While some projects were very small, others were major projects spanning several years. These were spread over the whole country. The projects that received grants may be divided roughly into projects:

- aimed at increasing interest in culture and broadening participation in cultural life;
- in which culture was used as an instrument to illustrate and initiate a discussion of workplace experience;
- aimed at documenting a workplace, an occupation or history of an occupational group;
- intended to promote a sense of community within a workplace.

In the future, responsibility for projects is to be taken by culture professionals, with a greater diversity of projects that generate a sense of art in everyday life, create new work opportunities for artists and improve the general working environment and health of workers. An increased spirit of community has been detected, together with an improved atmosphere in workplaces, the creation of new roles in the working community and the generation of creative capital.

Policies for Culture (Romania)

Policies for Culture is an initiative of the Ecumest Association in Romania, which aims at fostering access, democratisation and cultural democracy processes, as well as diversity and participation in central and eastern Europe. Funded by a number of European organisations and the ministries of culture of Bulgaria, Romania and Croatia, Ecumest runs several programmes and research initiatives. One of the programmes is called Policies for Culture, which "aims to encourage a participative principle in the design, implementation and evaluation of new effective cultural policies throughout South East Europe". The programme intends to bolster co-operation and information exchange and has also supported more than 20 projects to promote interaction and dialogue between citizens, the cultural sector and policy makers. Among the activities of the programme there are also research projects to provide independent information on existing policies and to draft recommendations for improvements. The programme website offers cultural policy information and the network aims to lobby for further action in the field of participative cultural policy making in the region.

Artemisszio Foundation (Hungary)

The Artemisszio Foundation promotes cultural diversity by encouraging dialogue between culturally, ethnically and socially diverse groups; it supports the social integration of disadvantaged groups and aims at strengthening international and European scientific and cultural relationships. Socially disadvantaged groups are a priority in the foundation's activities. The resources section of the website contains publications on subjects including international and national youth work, cultural anthropology, interculturality, civil society and youth affairs. The foundation has as its goals to:

– encourage continuous dialogue and interaction between culturally, ethnically and socially diverse groups and to foster their mutual understanding;
– support the social integration of socially and culturally disadvantaged groups;
– strengthen scientific and cultural relations internationally;
– develop and disseminate intercultural training courses, educational materials and methods.

The foundation organises courses for minority – especially youth – groups in local municipalities. During these courses, the young people learn about conflicts in ethnic and cultural groups in order to recognise, analyse and handle them in culture. As operational tools, the organisation uses art, theatre and other cultural instruments. The mission of the foundation is to provide an opportunity for the widest possible section of society to take part in activities that develop competencies that strengthen relations among people, improve communication and conflict-resolution skills, and contribute to the development of tolerance, mutual understanding and co-operation. It is a priority to include socially disadvantaged groups – the unemployed, people living in rural areas, the Roma and immigrants – to increase their equal opportunities and to fight social exclusion.

Creative Partnerships programme (United Kingdom)

Facilitating children's and young people's access to culture and artistic creation is a general objective of European cultural policies. The right to education is a fundamental right expressed in practically every European constitution, and offering children and young people meaningful cultural experiences is an important policy principle derived from it.

Arts Council England manages a Creative Partnerships programme for schools and young people funded by the government through the Department of Children, School and Families and the Department for Culture, Media and Sport. This programme focuses on the most deprived communities in England and "enables head teachers to realise their personal vision for a school, freeing them up to innovate and succeed. It encourages an approach designed around the needs of the individual school with learning tailored to the needs and aspirations of each child."

The programme seeks to develop the:

- creativity of young people, raising their aspirations and achievements;
- skills of teachers and their ability to work with creative practitioners;
- schools' approaches to culture, creativity and partnership working;
- skills, capacity and sustainability of the creative industries.

The programme enables young people to develop their creative skills and have a natural introduction to cultural participation and expression. In order to answer this demand, the first step is to develop a school improvement plan together with the schools in order to map out the main issues that need to be addressed. In this, the participatory process and co-operation with creative professionals are the main goals, rather than the result, in order to establish a long-term relationship. The programme identifies the appropriate creative professionals or practitioners. The management is never arbitrary but aims at using careful planning, research, training and identification of appropriate collaborators.

More than 550 000 students had participated in the programme at the time of writing and the results showed positive benefits for their academic performance. The programme has run in 36 areas in about 1 100 schools – however, through its different associated schemes (professional development for teachers and dissemination of best practices), it has reached one in three British schools.[53]

Project Europe, a campaign of the Austrian Ministry of Education, Science and Culture through KulturKontact Austria, is a similar initiative – a creative competition that stimulates creative and artistic teaching projects.

"Children's Jury" for reading promotion (Latvia)

In Latvia, the Culture Capital Foundation, under the auspices of the ministry of culture, offers programmes and support for participation activities. The foundation runs three specific programmes – two on theatre and one on children's literacy. The "Children's Jury" is the first part of a national reading promotion programme for children. The objective is to introduce children to various books and then encourage their critical thinking by inviting them to write about their favourite ones. At the end of the programme, there are several related events, from conferences with famous writers to children's parties. In 2003, 10 000 children and 397 libraries took part in the programme. Comparable initiatives have also been taking place in Estonia, Lithuania, Austria, Germany and Scandinavia.

---

53. More information can be found at: www.creative-partnerships.com.

Swiss Cultural Programme in the Western Balkans

On behalf of the Swiss Agency for Development and Co-operation, the Arts Council of Switzerland co-ordinates a programme called the Swiss Cultural Programme in the Western Balkans (SCP), aiming to promote democracy, respect minorities and build structures for broad cultural participation, especially in the case of young people. The programme has been designed for a five-year period (2007-12) and since the beginning of 2008 its focus has been on Albania, Bosnia and Herzegovina, "the former Yugoslav Republic of Macedonia", Serbia and Kosovo. Because of the entrance of Bulgaria and Romania into the European Union, their respective offices were closed in 2007. The programme is managed from Sarajevo with local offices in Belgrade, Skopje, Tirana and Pristina.

SCP consists of regional co-operation and "short-term projects, realised by local partner organisations and artists, to whom subsidiary project-specific contributions are granted to facilitate the development and implementation of cultural projects in a changing economic and social environment". The programme has an advisory board in each of the countries, which plans and makes decisions based on regional working guidelines. These are based on "a review of the activities in all programme countries, on the cultural context monitoring by the local boards and on the regional seminar with all local stakeholders (offices and boards) as well as representatives from headquarters and Pro Helvetia head office". SCP underlines that applicable projects must be run by citizens of the target countries or at least attract significant participation from them.

Fair culture (Finland)

In April 2005 the Finnish Ministry of Culture and Education launched a project on ethics in cultural policies to map policies from the cultural rights point of view. The objective was to identify ethical elements and to design guidelines for ethical cultural policies. The fields of analysis chosen were art and culture, heritage and communication and – as "applied" fields – the creative economy and the importance of art in well-being. The areas looked at included cultural traditions, lifestyles and identity, protection of diversity, vitality and continuity of culture, cultural infrastructures, access to and participation in cultural life, diversity of media, cultural consumption and cultural goods, diversity of cultural contents, ethnic and cultural diversity of minorities, social cohesion, cultural interaction, governance and cultural education.

Under the programme, agreements, declarations, legal frameworks, strategies and other texts were analysed. The first part of the project was to launch a debate at national level, for which the ministry organised a Seminar on Fair Culture in February 2006. The second phase was the publication of its results at the end of 2006. For the period between 2007 and 2010 several lines of action are recommended, from setting up a cultural policy ethics committee to developing indicators for ethical assessment of cultural policies. Fair culture is defined as "the realisation of cultural rights and the inclusion of everyone in cultural signification, irrespective of their age, gender, disability, or ethnic, religious and cultural background".

The ethical dimensions of cultural policy are:

– access to the tradition of humankind and one's own cultural sphere;
– physical, regional and cultural accessibility;
– the diversity and matching of cultural provision;
– cultural participation;
– opportunities for inclusion, and capability for cultural self-expression and signification.

The publication also suggests that each art and culture sector should review its own special features in relation to ethics in cultural policy.

Association of Independent Young Talent (Bulgaria)

The Association of Independent Young Talent (AIYT) is a national organisation specialised in children's and youth literature, with the aim of supporting young people to explore and develop their artistic potential. The association organises literature clubs called "Ikar" (with poetry, literature discussions and debates and seminars on poetry and literature) and disseminates the work of its members through a network of publishing houses and periodicals. The organisation recognises young talent through a nationwide competition for young poets and publication of their work through selected anthologies. Selected works are also published on the interactive web page of the association, where users are invited to evaluate the works through a ranking system.

Free access to museums (France)

In October 2007, the French Ministry of Culture and Communication announced the launch of a new programme on free access to museums. The main objective of this initiative is to know whether free access has an impact on the participation of the public in cultural activities. The ministry selected a number of museums and monuments in Paris and the rest of the country to form part of the initiative for six months – from January to the end of June 2008. At the beginning of the programme only access to permanent collections was free of charge. This is because several studies have shown that people who visit temporary collections are already frequent visitors to museums and other cultural activities. Under the second phase of the programme, action will be aimed more specifically at young people; four museums in Paris will offer free admission to those aged between 18 and 26 on one night a week.

The ministry of culture and communication will evaluate the initiative, looking at duration, conditions of the visits, frequency and the social and professional composition of the public in a comparative study. The results will determine whether this scheme should be extended to other museums and, most importantly, whether it has an impact on participation rates and the number of visits – above all in less-visited museums.

Several countries have adopted policies for free access to museums. In Poland a Law on Museums from 1966 established free access once a month and similar initiatives have, for example, been established in Greece, the United Kingdom (where most public museums are free all the time), Denmark and Estonia. Many countries use special passes for museums, such as the Swiss museum pass that makes more than 445 museums accessible.

In Sweden, the policy of free admission to museums was dropped in January 2007 after two successful years. Visits to museums dropped nearly 20% as a result. The ministry justified the action by explaining that entrance fees are needed to help finance the protection of Sweden's cultural heritage. The cultural affairs committee of the opposition has, however, argued that by "putting an end to free admission to museums, the government has limited the dissemination of Sweden's cultural heritage".

6. Measuring access, provision and participation in cultural life

When drafting policy, the question is raised as to whether the actions taken have the intended impact, whether they reach the target groups and result in more favourable conditions for everyone. How should the expected outcome be measured? What indicators should be used to measure individuals' access to cultural rights or participation in cultural life? How can strengthening it contribute to social inclusion and participation?

In order to measure these factors and build successful policies based on evidence, there is a clear need to develop indicators that offer quantitative and qualitative information on participation as well as evaluation and monitoring. Indicators are not simply statistics but tools for devising policies and planning strategies for further action. In an ideal case indicators help to condense complex issues into an easily understandable format. There is a need for indicators at local and regional level to show how cultural communities understand the social effects of culture, since our cultural understanding defines how we see and how we feel about our role in society. But there is also a need for indicators at state level. Countries want reliable information on the effects and success of their policies. Different sources indicate different characteristics that indicators should have – from coherence to relevance and availability.

Catherine Murray (2003) suggests that the interest elicited in the 1990s in mapping and designing participatory cultural policies was due to three convergent trends: growing dissatisfaction with the reliability and utility of measurement methods; the value and ideological basis of responding better to demand; and the emerging theoretical concern to bring cultural policies closer to the people. In her study of cultural participation, she sees three main problems: how to measure access, how to define consumption or participation and how to place cultural participation in the context of everyday life. Murray says that to measure access is difficult as there is no consensus on the forms of cultural life or cultural activities that one needs to have access to. However, she says that measuring cultural participation enables governments to decide how to extend a sense of cultural citizenship.

In the 1990 there was great interest in developing indicators on culture and cultural participation. As a part of finding cultural indicators for development, Lourdes Arizpe identified three issues: participation in creative activity, access to culture, and repositioning culture – conviviality. According to Sakiko Fukuda-Parr, these issues are related to questions concerning equity of conditions of participation in cultural expression and access to creative activities by different groups; our own and those of others. The last issue is related to the space for individuals and communities to express their culture, and respect related to the co-existence of different expressions. Along the same idea of development, culture and indicators, Terry McKinley suggested the construction of a cultural freedom index, or a cultural empowerment index, which would include the number of people directly and indirectly involved in creative activity.

As reported in many sources, attempts to develop sets of indicators are various and often unrelated. The report published by IFACCA (International Federation of Arts Councils and Culture Agencies) on "Statistical indicators for arts policy" in 2005 draws a general picture of the processes and concludes that cultural indicators are largely underdeveloped – and that different approaches hinder the adoption of universal indicators. The IFACCA report also presents useful information on continuing processes, a bibliography and key issues in the field of cultural indicators, including the main problems, as well as guidance on "what makes a good indicator".[54]

There are several studies on the social impact of arts, culture or participation (as already mentioned under 2.3). Joshua Guetzkow offers a good overview in his paper "How the arts impact communities: an introduction to the literature on arts impact studies" (2002). UNESCO has an excellent track record in setting standards related to cultural indicators, as shown in its *Our creative diversity* (report of the World Commission on Culture and Development, which included a set of standards for evaluating processes), and its World Culture Reports 1998 and 2000; and it also proposed six indicator areas from 1998 that include access to culture (as related to whether groups have access to the creativity of others) and participation (participation of groups in creative activities). Eurocult21 has developed indicators related to participation in cities, and the Cultures and Globalisation series presents a large set of general cultural indicators, some of which can be useful in measuring cultural opportunities or participation in cultural activities.

134

54. A good indicator is above all grounded in theory, relevant, linked to policy practice, comparable across regions and time, measurable, easily understood and clear, among other things (IFACCA).

ERICarts holds an impressive collection of data from different European countries. As mentioned before, the authors make a distinction between "attendance" and "consumption" of cultural goods and services, and propose a possible indicator in order to compare the level of access to some goods and services in different countries: Cupix (prices for selected popular cultural goods and services). The objective is to compare the average price of different cultural goods and services, such as books, movie tickets, and others. Bina (2006) notes that the results of the Cupix comparison could prove useful for measuring access to culture if comparative information on the income or minimum wage was included. Other useful sources include work on the development of cultural indicators by Matarasso (2001), Duxbury, Simons and Warfield (2003), Bonet (2004), Schuster (2002), and Anheier and Yudhishthir (2007), conference papers from international conferences (International Symposium on Culture Statistics, Montreal, October 2002; the International Seminar on Cultural Indicators, Mexico, 2003), work by the Task Force on Cultural Indicators of Human Development in Africa, 2004, and others) and mapping exercises in countries outside Europe (such as the cultural cartography in Chile and cultural indicator processes in Colombia and Argentina).

Better indicators of participation and improved cultural statistics on it are needed too. The criticism of current systems is that participation data mainly reflects attendance and is not comparative or complete. The data is not, and maybe cannot be, compared at international level due to differences between systems and structures. There is considerable scepticism about the accuracy of universal indicators or of overall comparison between countries. Vladimir Bina (2006) says that "to expect that all member states of the Council of Europe can provide data and indicators on the supply of, access to and participation in culture in their own country would be an illusion. The best we can hope for are partial comparisons for a limited number of countries. Such comparisons will consist of quantitative data (although these are not always harmonised and thus not strictly speaking comparable) and best practices." Bina suggests the Compendium of Cultural Policies and Trends in Europe, with its existing data and structure, as a starting point. He also refers to the fact that many surveys show a correlation between cultural participation and involvement in civil society.

In his 2002 book, *Towards cultural citizenship: tools for cultural policy and development*, Colin Mercer offers useful indicator clusters that are listed in four categories:

- cultural vitality, diversity and conviviality (cultural economy; production and consumption; cultural ecology);

- cultural access, participation and consumption;
- culture, lifestyle and identity;
- culture, ethics, governance and conduct.

On the second category, Mercer writes: "a minimum condition for this area of investment in the cultural field is the sort of aggregate data on participation in cultural activities, consumption of cultural products and services, that many national cultural ministries and agencies and many international agencies now collect and present". However, he also reminds us that, "what we need to know most about access, participation and consumption are not just aggregate numbers of watchers, listeners, consumers, participants (crucial as these are) but also how people are using these cultural forms to various ends of, for example, identity affirmation, personal development, social distinction and demarcation, etc. and how these various uses are articulated to socio-economic and other demographic variables." The clusters Mercer proposes are closely linked to each other and present a clear picture of what they intend to clarify.

When it comes to indicators of the impact of cultural activities on the creation of social cohesion, and the impact of cultural activities in local communities, several studies exist. Fisher (2001) refers to the list of social results of artistic projects with the participation of citizens in Northern Ireland drawn up by the think tank Comedia. Fisher adds indicators to the Comedia list: the number of cultural activities related to civil society themes, the number of cultural associations in the voluntary sector, the number of self-sustained cultural organisations, the demographic profile of the participants, the number of voluntary organisations in a community, the infrastructure capacity to support local groups and the number of participatory cultural opportunities within five kilometres of each citizen.

The UNDP's "Governance indicators: a users' guide" (2004) underlines that indicators can help in promoting accountability, transparency and empowerment of citizens, and are essential tools for devising policies and strategies on cultural inclusion. The indicators on cultural participation should not only include information on participation in cultural services but should categorise people's needs in relation to co-existence and community development, including opportunities for participation, creation of services and cultural activities. There is a lack of indicators on the impact on quality of life and personal growth of the groups in danger of social and cultural exclusion.

For the realisation of cultural rights, the following list of questions was used in a comparative study of European countries carried out by the Interarts Foundation in 2006. It mapped out existing initiatives, programmes and legal processes in four different European countries:

- legislation on cultural rights, access and participation;
- cultural rights in governmental and administrative plans and measures;
- the visibility of cultural rights in national cultural administration;
- the national, regional and local understanding of cultural rights;
- initiatives related to cultural rights;
- the right for groups with special needs to participate in cultural life – at the legal and administrative level;
- the rights of immigrants and ethnic minorities;
- international instruments;
- national, regional and local programmes;
- other themes of interest (cultural cohesion, immigration, etc.);
- cultural rights and their development.

United Cities and Local Governments (UCLG), the organisation behind drafting Agenda 21 for Culture, has also called for more research on participation in culture at the local level. It proposes a "policy framework to explain local cultural policies" as being more relevant than the production of a set of indicators at this point. The "framework of qualitative indicators on cultural policies" includes a list of 28 items for the self-evaluation of local cultural policies.

The paper commissioned by the Division of Cultural Policies and Intercultural Dialogue of UNESCO from the Working Group on Culture of UCLG presents some possible indicators on cultural diversity at the local level, derived from three experts' papers. Some of these indicators are related to access and participation, such as mapping needs and priorities (the three policy areas citizens tend to find relevant or important), physical access to cultural services (cultural centres and organisations but also cultural events and activities in hospitals, prisons, schools, day-care centres, and residences for elderly people), the presence of arts and cultural plans or policies that support a diversity of expression and encourage public use of urban space, and economic and fiscal resources, among others.

**Access, participation and cultural provision in the framework of cultural rights –
A proposal for indicator fields or evaluation of a cultural rights approach to policy[55]**

	Legal development (structural)	Administrative level (process)
Access to and participation in cultural life (national)	*National legislation:* – existence of legislative instruments (constitution or other) on access to and participation in culture	Existence of policies, structures (programmes, administrative actors), policy priorities, and policy strategies on access and participation
Access to and participation in cultural life (regional and local)	*National legislation:* – existence of legislative instruments on local and regional cultural administration – existence and nature of local and regional regulations and normative non-binding tools	*Decentralisation:* – existence of measures of cultural competence carried out by local and regional actors *Structures:* – existence of regional and local policies, structures (programmes, administrative actors), and policy strategies on access and participation
Access to and participation in cultural life (international)	*International instruments:* ratification (number and nature of, and organisation) Participation in international legal processes and initiatives	Existence, number, nature and geographic scope of international cultural co-operation projects Existence of funding opportunities for international cultural co-operation
Specific groups (people with disabilities, minorities, women, groups in danger of social exclusion, people in institutions, children and young people)	Legislation related to access and participation of specific groups	Existence of policies, structures (programmes, administrative actors), policy priorities, and policy strategies on access and participation of specific groups
Cultural offer	*National legislation:* – existence of normative instruments on the quality and contents of the cultural offer – existence of normative instruments on media and arts instruments for specific groups	Existence of evaluation or other participatory processes on the (needs and necessities) as regards the cultural offer Existence of quotas or other measures

55. This section benefits from work developed with Dr Yvonne Donders on cultural indicators of development and human rights (2009).

Civil society (outcome)	Cultural institutions (process/outcome)
Existence, number and nature of national cultural actors of the civil society (cultural associations, volunteer organisations, third sector actors, platforms, movements)	Existence of operational tools or strategies for fostering access to and participation in culture Studies on operational principles
Existence, number and nature of regional and local cultural actors of the civil society (cultural associations, volunteer organisations, third sector actors, platforms, movements)	Existence, number and nature of cultural institutions at local and regional level Existence, number and nature of programmes and initiatives for cultural participation of the local/regional public
Existence, number, nature and geographic scope of international cultural co-operation projects of non-state actors (should be based on a mapping exercise and research)	Existence, number, nature and geographic scope of international cultural co-operation projects of cultural institutions (should be based on a mapping exercise and research)
Mapping of the cultural needs and necessities of specific groups	Existence, number and nature of cultural activities for and on specific groups Mapping of the expectations of the attending public
Mapping of the cultural "offer" of civil society actors Evaluation of the "personal" motivation in participating in the activities of cultural third sector/civil society actors	Evaluation of the offer of cultural institutions Research on attendance, ticket sales, evaluation periods, trends Mapping of the expectations of the attending public

	Legal development (structural)	Administrative level (process)
Civil society	Legislation and normative instruments related to funding of civil society and cultural organisations	Existence of policies, structures (programmes, administrative actors), policy priorities, and policy strategies on civil society actors
Evaluation	Evaluation of the progress of national constitutional law	Evaluation of policies, programmes, projects and other initiatives
Participatory processes and decision making	Existence of normative instruments of participatory processes	Existence of initiatives, channels or consultation groups or other structures (web pages, etc.) that facilitate the participation of the public in decision-making processes
Linguistic rights	Existence of normative instruments on linguistic rights and culture	Existence of policies, structures (programmes, administrative actors), policy priorities, and policy strategies on linguistic rights
Access to heritage	Existence of normative instruments on access to heritage	Existence of policies, structures (programmes, administrative actors), policy priorities, policy strategies on access to heritage
Access to other cultures	Existence of normative instruments of access to other cultures	Existence of policies, structures (programmes, administrative actors), policy priorities, and policy strategies on access to information on other cultures
Mobility and exchange	Existence of normative instruments on mobility and exchange	Existence of policies, structures (programmes, administrative actors), policy priorities, and policy strategies on mobility and exchange
Research and training		Existence of infrastructure for research (statistics, studies) in the field Existence of policies, programmes and projects on training

Civil society (outcome)	Cultural institutions (process/outcome)
Impact studies and evaluation of the activities of third sector actors Mapping of the "personal" impact on taking part in "cultural" civil society	Existence of joint projects and other contacts with civil society actors
Evaluation of the activities of civil society actors and the outcome – if their actions have facilitated access to culture	Evaluation of the activities of cultural institutions and the outcome – if their actions have facilitated access to culture
Participation of civil society actors (organisations, platform) in decision-making processes and consultation groups	Participation of professionals in the cultural sector in decision-making processes and consultation groups
Use of lesser-used, regional and minority languages in civil society organisations	Information on the cultural offer of institutions on lesser-used, regional and minority languages
	Number of cultural institutions in the field of heritage Physical access to cultural heritage sites
Existence of information channels and structures on cultural information Access to cultural expressions of a "foreign" culture	Existence, number and nature of cultural activities/offer (exhibitions, concerts, plays, etc.) of "other" cultures
Number of people taking part in exchange programmes	Existence of professional mobility programmes or exchange information Participation of cultural professionals in international conferences
Training courses for civil society actors on relevant issues (cultural rights, strategies, minority cultures, etc.)	Training of personnel of cultural institutions on relevant issues (cultural rights, strategies, minority cultures, etc.)

What, then, could be possible indicators on access, participation in cultural life and fulfilment of cultural rights, based on the information above? Recently the author has asked this question in every training course where she gave a lecture. How would the students measure participation and cultural rights in their field (if related to the cultural sector) or in official policy? There have been a variety of answers, including surprisingly accurate and innovative forms of evaluation. The answers have varied from the construction of new theatres, museums and exhibition spaces to an annual subscription to the national authors' rights organisation – and from calculating the benefit of subsidised theatre production by number of visitors, to the financial balance of popular festivals and calculating how many productions can be carried out with public money and how few without it. Some have even said that the "sense of change or impact" after a cultural experience for someone who had no previous means of participating is already an indicator. Believing in the power of culture, one can hardly disagree, even if it is difficult to translate emotions into figures.

Proposing a list of indicators is a risky undertaking since systems, methods and realities are different. It seems that we are not yet ready for the use of indicators but are still at the stage of deciding in which fields one really needs information. The human rights indicators propose a helpful organisation of structural, process and outcome indicators, which are explored through a 4A system (availability, accessibility, acceptability and adaptability.) Following the example of the authors of Agenda 21 for Culture, the following is presented simply as a checklist and not yet as a list of permanent indicators.

7. Trends and conclusions

We can agree or disagree about whether cultural participation may or may not give a deeper meaning to our lives or equip us to have a say in the decisions that affect our opportunities. We might think that access to culture and participation in cultural life enlarges our sense of being part of a community and gives emotional meaning to our social interaction. We might need more information on who and what makes up the culture we live in and how we ourselves participate in its constitution. As we know, culture is not a static fact but a living organism and therefore our ways of participating also go through changes. What we probably all agree on is that we should be given the opportunity to have access, we should be able to choose whether or not to participate, and that all this should have a regulatory basis that ensures this in any given circumstances and to everyone. Public policies, especially cultural policies, should reflect and contribute to the construction of an enabling environment where rights to access to and participation in cultural life are covered.

This means that every citizen, whether a member of a majority or a minority, has the same rights. In practice, however, the power that many international treaties have may turn out to be quite modest. But international law does provide some of the most important parameters that have a bearing on the realisation of access and participation. They reflect a consensus of the international community on these issues and therefore it is important that countries participate in international processes. The real test, however, always comes on the home front – showing how international (and national) regulations are turned into inclusive policies.

The legal development in Europe in terms of cultural participation rights reveals that older constitutions include less cultural aspects whereas more recent constitutions have taken them more into account. The explanation is fairly simple; legal development, political changes and understanding of human rights procedures have progressed. The cultural rights references mostly concern fundamental freedoms and human rights, or educational aspects, although some newer constitutions include references to cultural rights and participation in cultural life. But even though legal development has progressed, policies have not always followed. So they might not be inclusive or innovative enough but follow well-worn paths.

Interestingly, some countries that do not have a strong legal framework assuring participation have still adopted successful policies and approaches to foster it, and countries that may have strong cultural participation principles in theory may have not successfully translated them into adequate action.

What becomes clear is that there is a need for strong legal development of participatory cultural rights as a base for policies. The most common approaches are directed to action such as establishing a library network, ensuring inexpensive or free access to museums (or other cultural services) or organising arts education for children and young people. There are a variety of successful actions but there also seems to be a lack of policies directed at elderly people or towards the public in general. An exciting example of how policy can be made to operate successfully is the Swedish experience on culture in working life, which aims to advance cultural democracy by involving people without previous artistic experience in activities.

Cultural legislation in many European countries clearly needs to be modernised. This means not only developing a general legal framework for cultural participation but also specific regulations that respond to the needs of different sectors of the public. At the same time more research is needed on cultural legislation and regulations at different administrative levels in order to have a clearer picture of the special features of each sector and country. Making people part of legislative processes is important as it makes them more transparent. The Scottish example of restructuring the cultural administration according to certain rights and public consultation on the Culture Bill, or the Finnish example of making culture "fair and just" for everyone, shows a remarkable will to not only make culture, but also cultural policies, more accessible to people. Because this is what cultural and public policies are about; they are about people.

The cultural sector is very vulnerable to budgetary changes and when times get rough countries tend to limit cultural resources. Making policies successful is often about time, resources and money. The lack of financial resources is an easy way to explain that, while there is no real lack of interest, other issues take priority over cultural participation in the list for immediate action. Few can argue that cultural participation is more important than a functioning social security system or that cultural rights are more important than the right to housing, health care or education. Cultural rights seem an easy target in these confrontational situations even if there is no real conflict between the issues. Keeping cultural rights in the margin of human rights and keeping culture in the margin of the development of participatory policies means maintaining an elitist vision of culture – namely that expression, creativity and enjoyment of cultural opportunity remains a privilege of well-educated high-earning citizens. There is substantial work to be done on cultural rights, access and participation, and this work deserves not only a good legal support system, but also better resources, visibility and official recognition.

There is also a need to know more about participation and its different forms in order to make better policies. Most participation studies concentrate on registering the attendance of different groups and following the trends of attendance rates. At this point, it might not even be too important to be able to carry out international comparisons but to know more about the impact of domestic cultural policies and the needs of the users of cultural services. Evaluating the effectiveness of cultural policies for the target group may prove to be more successful in the long run than comparing different cultural realities. International comparative studies give valuable information on the possibility of adapting different models, but it is important to know how groups from minorities, elderly people, women and families feel their cultural participation rights are secured – and how public administrations respond to their differing needs. Several studies have shown that there is a lack of information on the translation of rights into policies. Sometimes evaluations take place but there is too often a complete lack of systematic analysis.

Cultural rights are basically about access and inclusion and for successful cultural policies a cultural rights approach to policy making will be useful even if a critical evaluation is always needed. Development of legislation is not only the task of cultural administrations but consultation is always important. Often minority groups feel that they are kept too far away from decision-making processes and that decisions are not made by them but for them. The same observation can be made in the case of young audiences that remain distanced from official cultural policies and so establish their own subculture forums. At the same time, European cultural policies seem to have turned their back on the growing group of elderly people that are in great need of tailored cultural services. All these different groups need their own approaches and regulations that give them the chance to participate. Cultural participation is an issue of political will and good governance. In some countries the attempts to establish task forces to set basic standards of cultural services or to ensure a more participatory touch in cultural policies has barely begun, partly due to changes of administration.

Europe has a large community of third sector and civil society organisations that need support, resources, cultural autonomy and trust. Successful cultural policies should be drafted in collaboration with organisations and associations dealing with groups with special needs and should acknowledge the role of the civil society.

In the conclusions of the 2002 Barcelona Seminar on the Right to Take Part in Cultural Life, civil society representatives, not surprisingly, underlined the need to connect the micro-level (local) with the macro-level (international). They pointed out that waiting for big international organisations to act does not solve problems in the development of cultural rights and the social dimension of culture. The public tend to mistrust not only the execution of policies and the fulfilment of policy objectives, but also the functioning of international instruments.

As Jordi Pascual i Ruiz (2007) says: "the recognition of the link between culture and human rights, and therefore the central place of culture in attaining full human development, opens the door to public responsibility, and thus the need for cultural policies to walk the fine line from 'raw capacities' to 'capabilities' to 'activities'. More than ever, contemporary phenomena require a personal analysis that can only be provided by access to, and practice with, cultural activities. If freedom and development involve culture, therefore, the public institutions need to find the laws and the policies, and later on the programmes and the projects, to guarantee that all citizens/inhabitants can attain, with and through culture, full human development. Cultural policies are said to create the opportunities that no other public sphere provides."

A citizen may be aware in general of the importance of participation in cultural life and the importance of human – including cultural – rights, but may not necessarily always fully experience what this means in his or her own life. The Belgian example is an illustrative case of how different participation dynamics (and obstacles) can be mapped and later evaluated for their impact on target groups. There is a need to know more about participation in general and in relation to popular culture, language, integration of education and cultural programmes, technological advances and cultural programmes, and other issues.

Public administrations in European countries tend to look for ways to give direct or indirect support to minority organisations. Mostly this means financial support. Countries that have a long history of interculturalism involving minorities in cultural policy making have made some advances but there are others that are still learning to find ways to improve minorities' levels of cultural participation. Even though different social groups may share some common characteristics in their channels of access to culture, the criteria designed to reach them may not be universal, and may require a range of funding models.

In many countries, the budget allocations for cultural participation activities are rarely designed for self-sufficient or long-term projects. The tendency to rely on project-based funding limits the continuity of activities and is an obstacle to long-term results. Short-term thinking may be successful in obtaining immediate results but can make it more difficult to sustain engagement. A majority of the projects that address social inclusion through arts and culture are established as civil society initiatives with funding from the public sector. And while the cultural projects on offer to people with low incomes or ethnic minorities are quite substantial in many places, there is still inadequate co-ordination of the initiatives, communication and information. The lack of financial resources, global vision and political coherence at times explains the relative isolation of cultural operators who often wish to have more inter-institutional and inter-sectorial collaboration.

There could be far better systems for the exchange of experiences, and for training cultural and other public administrators on cultural rights issues. More recognition needs to be given, as well, to the transversal role of culture in the social agenda. For Eduard Delgado, for example, a secure society is one in which all citizens not only have the right to information but also the right to be heard. George Yúdice (2006) says that a secure society "implies a public sphere permeable to all, one which includes everyone's heritage. Only thus can quality of life be ensured for all."

8. Improving policy

We are faced with the question of how to translate legal instruments, principles and indicators into effective policy; how to shape participation in the context of daily life, to tackle tensions arising from shared space and from the fight for limited resources. How should we try to make everyone happy? The last question seems easiest to answer for policy makers, who know that answering every need is an impossible task. Making cultural provision universal, though, can be achieved. In doing so, conditions should be met and principles respected. One of these conditions is equity – meaning a real fulfilment of equal opportunities, with suitable products and information to achieve it. Policy should be based on values and principles that have equity, non-discrimination and dignity at their root.

Catherine Murray (2003) asks whether actions to encourage participation automatically deliver equity and social cohesion. However, since the intention is to create opportunities, whether social inclusion and equity automatically result is almost beside the point. Initiatives that animate society and allow people to articulate their own priorities may prove to be the most successful in the long run. They spread the idea of everyone's shared responsibility to create a space for cultural co-existence – especially at a time when traditional forms of cultural participation are being expanded with new forms that change our understanding of what better policy consists of.

Choosing between options when resources are limited and selection has to be made is never easy. However, at least the basic elements of access to and participation in cultural life must be covered. The following list provides some ideas and direction on how countries could plan and carry out initiatives for a cultural rights approach to cultural policies.

It is important to promote research and discussion. As this study shows, there is still a lack of information on many issues. There is a need for traditional and non-traditional studies on participation: attendance, ticket sales, evaluation periods, trends, civil society actors, cultural institutions, political attitudes, public opinion, virtual participation, etc. The Council of Europe's Compendium of Cultural Policies and Trends in Europe has proved to be a very useful tool in comparing cultural policies in Europe. There is a need for a compendium tool or chapter on the:

– participation in cultural life of disabled people;

– participation in cultural life of national, ethnic and linguistic minorities;

– participation in cultural life in prisons, hospitals, elderly homes and schools;

– civil society actors and third sector keyholders;

– virtuality and virtual participation.

There is a need for cultural policies that answer the needs of "users". Young people need strategies and activities that reflect the reality of their lives. Cultural minorities need possibilities to maintain cultural traditions as well as to participate in the culture of the majority. Cultural policies become more successful when patronisation is avoided and participation fostered. Cultural policies need to be thematic, sectorial and cohesive. Cultural policies should be innovative, risk-taking and participatory. There is a need for participatory policy instruments designed in collaboration with citizens and with organisations and associations of special needs groups.

There is a need for fostering dialogue between different actors. There is a need for space where cultural networks, and civil society associations and organisations can meet, virtually or in person. There is a need for interdisciplinary networking and co-operation. There is a need to define goals and priorities together.

There is a need to make successful experiences more visible and accessible, to know more about local experiences and to explore initiatives run by third sector and civil society organisations, cities and local administration. There is need to know who does what and who is who.

There is need to have better and more accurate statistics. There is a need for periodical mapping of national cultural circumstances in order to deal with current challenges. There is a need for more information on the number of NGOs active in the field of access to and participation in cultural life (mapping), financing of civil society actors, impact studies and evaluation of action of NGOs, voluntary organisations, amateur arts participation and its impact on personal life.

There is a need for capacity-building for professionals working in the cultural sector, interdisciplinary networking within the cultural sector and long-term support for programmes and initiatives. There is a need to include cultural rights in cultural education programmes.

There is a need for good legal instruments and follow-up of their implementation. There is a need for international, inter-sectorial and inter-institutional collaboration on themes related to access and participation in cultural life. There is a need for public debate.

This study pretends to be what it is; a fast train through a general landscape without stopping in detail. Its purpose is not to provide all the answers or information but to whet the appetite to explore more access, participation and cultural provisions in Europe. Access to and participation in culture are fundamental elements in a democracy and effective policy making, but above all they help in achieving a dignified and rich life.

References and selected bibliography

Adams, Don and Goldbard, Arlene

(2001), *Creative community. The art of cultural development*, Rockefeller Foundation, New York.

Anheier, Helmut Isar and Yudhishthir Raj

(2007), *Conflicts and tensions*, Cultures and globalization series, Vol. 1, Sage Publications.

Bamford, Anne

(2007), "Building participation and relevance in arts and cultural education", available at: www.educacao-artistica.gov.pt/interven%C3%A7%C3%B5es/Confer%C3%AAncia%20Anne%20Bamford.pdf.

Bianchini, Franco

(2005), "Reflections on standard setting in relation to issues of cultural provision, access and participation", Council of Europe, Steering Committee for Culture, CDCULT(2005)24, 24 October 2005.

Bina, Vladiminir

(2006), "Cultural provision, access and participation. A survey of data sources and qualitative indicators. Draft for Discussion", Council of Europe consultation meeting in December 2006.

Boccacin, Lucia

(2004), *The third sector in Italy: culture and practices*, Department of Sociology, Catholic University of Milan.

Bonet, Lluís

(2004), "Reflexiones a propósito de indicadores y estadísticas culturales", *Gestión Cultural*, No 7, available at: www.gestioncultural.org/gc/boletin/pdf/Indicadores/LBonet-Indicadores.pdf.

Bunting, Catherine

(2007), "Public value and the arts in England: discussion and conclusion of the arts debate", Arts Council England.

Butsenko, Olexandr

(2006), "Culture and democracy and the role of civil society in Ukraine", Council of Europe consultation meeting in December 2006.

Carámbula, Gonzalo

(2004) "South, cultural diversity and beyond" presented at the International Seminar on Diversity and Cultural Rights, Sao Paolo, 31 March.

Dietachmair, Philipp

(2007) *Guide to Citizen Participation in Local Cultural Policy Development for European Cities*, Interarts Foundation, ECUMEST Association, European Cultural Foundation.

Donders, Yvonne

(2004a), "The legal framework of the right to take part in cultural life", background document to the Dialogue on Cultural Rights and Human Development, Barcelona 2004.

(2004b), "Towards a right to cultural identity in international human rights law", presented at the International Seminar on Diversity and Cultural Rights, Sao Paolo, 31 March.

(2002), *Towards a right to cultural identity*, School of Human Rights Research, Vol. 14, Intersentia, Antwerp.

Dragićević Šešić, Milena

(2009), *Glossary on Access to Culture* for the Civil Society Platform on Access to Culture

(2001), *Cultural policies in eastern and central Europe*, Belgrade University.

Duxbury, Nancy, Simons, Derek and Warfield, Katie

(2006), "Local policies and expressions of cultural diversity: Canada and the United States", paper commissioned by the Institut de Cultura, Barcelona City Council in the framework of the study "Local policies for cultural diversity" commissioned by the Division of Cultural Policies and Intercultural Dialogue of UNESCO.

(2003), *Cultural indicators and benchmarks in community indicator projects: performance measures for cultural investment?* Canada Strategic Research and Analysis, Department of Canadian Heritage.

Eide, Asbjørn

(2002), "Minority rights and the right to participate in cultural life. With special reference to CECSR Article 15 (1) (a)", presented at the International Round Table on the Right to Take Part in Cultural Life, Quezon City, the Philippines, 11-13 February, 2002.

Ellmeier, Andrea

(2000), National report Austria, study for the Council of Europe, prepared by Österreichische Kultur-dokumentation, Internationales Archiv für Kulturanalysen, Vienna.

Engelhardt, Richard

(2006), "Cultural liberty and freedom of expression: lessons from Asian experience", presented at the International Forum of Cultural Rights and Diversity, 14-15 November, 2006, Seoul, Korean National Commission for UNESCO, Korean Culture and Tourism Policy, Interarts Foundation.

Fink-Hafner, Danica and Kustex-Lipicer, Simona

(2003), "Monitoring and evaluating cultural policies in Europe – The role of cultural statistics", paper prepared for the Hawaii International Conference on Statistics, 5-8 June 2003, Honolulu, Hawaii.

Fisher, Rod

(2001), *Culture and civil society: new relationships with the third sector*, Council of Europe Publishing, Strasbourg.

Fitzerald, Sandy (ed.)

(2004), *An outburst of frankness – Community arts in Ireland – A reader*, New Island.

Foote, John A.

(2006), "Culture and democracy", background paper prepared for the Council of Europe.

Fukuda-Parr, Sakiko

(2001), "In search of indicators of culture and development: review of progress and proposals for next steps", text prepared for the World Culture Report, 2001 edition.

Gottesdiener, Hana and Vilatte, Jean-Christophe

(2006), *L'accès des jeunes adultes à l'art contemporain. Approches sociologique et psychologique du goût des étudiants por l'art et leur fréquentation des musées.*

Guetzkow, Joshua

(2002), "How the arts impact communities: an introduction to the literature on arts impact studies", paper prepared for the Conference on Taking the Measure of Culture, 7-8 June 2002, Princeton University, New Jersey.

Hansen, Stephen A.

(2001), "The right to take part in cultural life: towards minimum core obligations related to Article 15 (1) (a) of the International Covenant on Economic, Social and Cultural Rights", draft, American Association for the Advancement of Science, Washington DC.

Hersent, Jean-François

(2003), "Les pratiques culturelles adolescents, France, début du troisième millénaire", For more information: http://cat.inist.fr/?aModele=afficheN&cpsidt=14842726.

Hewison, Robert and Holden, John

(2004), *The right to art: making aspirations reality*, DEMOS report.

Holden, John

(2007), *Logging on. Culture, participation and the web*, Demos.

(2006), *Cultural value and the crisis of legitimacy*, Demos.

Huysmans, Frank, van den Broek, Andries and de Haan, Jos

(2005), *Culture-lovers and culture-leavers. Trends in interest in the arts & cultural heritage in the Netherlands*, Social and Cultural Planning Office, Ministry of Education, Culture and Science.

Ilczuk, Dorota

(2001), *Cultural citizenship. Civil society and cultural policy in Europe*, Boekman Studies.

Khan, Naseem

(2006), "The combination of many voices", paper presented at the International Forum of Cultural Rights and Diversity, 14-15 November 2006, Seoul, Korean National Commission for UNESCO, Korean Culture and Tourism Policy, Interarts Foundation.

Kymlinka, Will

(2005), "A European experiment in protecting cultural rights", Human Rights Dialogue, special issue on cultural rights, Carnegie Council on Ethics and International Affairs, spring, Series 2, Number 12.

Laaksonen, Annamari

(2007), "Cultural rights, policies and participation", in *Training in management and cultural policies for cultural diversity and development*, publication of the international seminar, 30 August-2 September 2004, Documenta Universitaria.

(2006), "Building cohesion: cultural rights and their application into policies and action", paper presented at the International Forum of Cultural Rights and Diversity, 14-15 November 2006, Seoul, Korean National Commission for UNESCO, Korean Culture and Tourism Policy, Interarts Foundation.

(2005), "Measuring cultural exclusion through participation in cultural life", available at: www.comminit.com/en/node/219706/36.

Madden, Christopher

(2004), "Statistical indicators for arts policy. Discussion paper", IFACCA – International Federation of Arts Councils and Culture Agencies.

Magdowski, Iris Jane

(2006), "Tradition and Challenge Facing Political Europe: the European Example". International Forum on Cultural Rights and Diversity, organised by the Korean Commission for UNESCO, Korea Culture and Tourism Policy Institute and the Interarts Founcation, 14-15 November 2006, Seoul, Korea.

Marks, Stephen

(2003), "Defining cultural rights", in *Human rights and criminal justice for the downtrodden*, Martinus Nijhoff Publishers, Leiden/Boston, pp. 293-324.

(2002), "Definitional aspects of cultural rights", International Round Table on the Right to Take Part in Cultural Life, 11-13 February 2002, University of the Philippines.

Martin, Andy

(2003), *The impact of free entry to museums*, MORI.

Matarasso, François

(2001), "Cultural indicators: a preliminary review of issues raised by current approaches", Comedia. For more information: www.comedia.org.uk/index.htm.

(1997), "Use or ornament? The social impact of participation in the arts". For more information: www.comedia.org.uk/index.htm.

McKinley, Terry

(1997), *Cultural indicators of development*, UNRISD, UNESCO Occasional paper series on culture and development, UNESCO.

Mercer, Colin

(2005a), "Civitas: cities, cultures and citizenship", prepared for the Workshop on Cities and Citizenship: Developing Indicators of Cultural Diversity.

(2005b), "Cultural capital and capabilities: defining and measuring the cultural field", prepared for the Third Global Forum on Human Development, 17-19 January 2005.

(2002), *Towards cultural citizenship: tools for cultural policy and development*, Bank of Sweden Tercentenary Foundation and Sida, Hedemora and Stockholm.

Milevska, Suzana

"A paradigm shift from objects to subjects", available at: www.springerin.at/dyn/heft_text.php?textid=1761&lang=en, accessed 11 December 2009.

Mundy, Simon

(2000), *Cultural policy – A short guide*, Council of Europe Publishing, Strasbourg.

(1999), *Cultural rights and European democracies in transition*, Felix Meritis Papers No. 10, Gulliver, Amsterdam.

Murray, Catherine A.

(2003), "Cultural participation: toward a cultural policy paradigm", prepared for the Conference on Accounting for Culture: Examining the Building Blocks of Cultural Citizenship, sponsored by the Canadian Cultural Research Network, Department of Canadian Heritage, University of Ottawa.

(2002), "The third sector: cultural diversity and civil society", *Canadian Journal of Communication*, Vol. 27, pp. 331-350.

O'Toole, Fintan

(2006), "Dismantling the barriers to participation in cultural life", National Disability Authority, 5th National Research Conference, 16 November 2006, Dublin, available at: www.nda.ie/CntMgmtNew.nsf/dcc524b4546adb3080256c700071b049/5A19C972AF5A7B93802571E6 0052A06B/$File/3_fintan_otoole.htm, accessed 11 December 2009.

Pascual i Ruiz, Jordi

(2007), "On citizen participation in local cultural policy development for European cities", in *Guide to Citizen Participation in Local Cultural Policy Development for European Cities*, Interarts Foundation, ECUMEST Association, European Cultural Foundation.

Rudder, Pierce Antonio

(2006), "Cultural diversity and cultural expressions: why it is necessary to protect diversity", paper presented at the International Forum of Cultural Rights and Diversity, 14-15 November 2006, Seoul, Korean National Commission for UNESCO, Korean Culture and Tourism Policy, Interarts Foundation.

Schuster, J. Mark

(2007), "Participation studies and cross-national comparison: proliferation, prudence, and possibility", Cultural Trends, Vol. 16, No. 2, June 2007, pp. 99-196.

(2002), "Informing cultural policy – Data, statistics, and meaning", paper presented at the International Symposium on Culture Statistics, 21-23 October, Montreal.

Sengupta, Arjun

(2002), "Cultural rights and the right to development", paper presented at the International Round Table on the Right to Take Part in Cultural Life, 11-13 February 2002, University of the Philippines.

Skaliotis, Michail

(2002), *Key figures on cultural participation in the European Union*, Eurostat, Unit 3, Health, Education and Culture, Luxembourg.

Stamatopoulou, Elsa

(2004), "Why cultural rights now?", Carnegie Council, 29 September 2004, New York.

Stanley, Dick

(2007), *A reflection on the function of culture in building citizenship capacity*, Council of Europe Publishing, Strasbourg.

(2004), "Report of the proceedings of the IFACCA/ISSEC Research Workshop 'Looking for New Connections', Montreal, August 24-25, 2004".

Kim, Su-Kab

(2006) "The system and realization of cultural rights in the constitution" presented at the International Forum of Cultural Rights and Diversity, 14-15 November 2006, Seoul, Korean National Commission for UNESCO, Korean Culture and Tourism Policy, Interarts Foundation.

Vidal, Emilie

(2007) Mapping of existing studies on access and participation. Interarts Foundation.

Yúdice, George

(2006), "Systems of cultural support and cultural diversity: contradiction and recommendations", paper presented at the International Forum of Cultural Rights and Diversity, 14-15 November 2006, Seoul, Korean National Commission for UNESCO, Korean Culture and Tourism Policy, Interarts Foundation.

Access of young people to culture, Interarts Foundation, commissioned by the Youth Unit of the Education, Audiovisual and Culture Executive Agency of the European Commission, 2009/2010.

"Access to culture. The cultural needs and rights of individuals", Leicester's Cultural Strategy – "Diverse city: a vision for cultural life in Leicester", Leicester City Council, 2001.

"All talents count. A pilot inventory of national cultural policies and measures supporting cultural diversity", ERICarts, 2001.

"A national plan for human rights 2006-2009", Ministry of Justice, Sweden, 2006.

Compendium of Cultural Policies and Trends in Europe: country reports, Council of Europe and ERICarts, see www.culturalpolicies.net/web/index.php.

"Cultura y discapacidad. Normativa existente y panorama de las iniciativas del sector público en Francia", Interarts Foundation, July 2007.

"Cultural Commission final report", Cultural Commission of Scotland, 23 June 2005.

"Cultural indicators and Agenda 21 for Culture", United Cities and Local Governments – Working Group on Culture, October 2004.

"Cultural participation survey", The Urban Institute, Washington, 2003.

"Democratisation culturelle, diversité culturelle, cohésion sociale", *Culture & Recherche*, December 2005.

"Draft Charter on Cultural Rights and Commitments of the Citizen of Barcelona", Interarts Foundation and the Culture Institute of the Barcelona City Council, 2002.

"Draft Culture (Scotland) Bill. Consultation document", Scottish Executive, 14 December 2006.

"Europeans' participation in cultural activities. A Eurobarometer survey carried out at the request of the European Commission", Eurostat, 2002.

"Family friendly toolkit", Arts Council England, 2006. "Final report on PSA target 2 on take-up of cultural opportunities by people aged 20 and over from priority groups", Arts Council England, 2007.

"Focus on cultural diversity. Findings of a study carried out by the Office for National Statistics", December 2003.

Human Development Report 2004, *Cultural liberty in today's' diverse world*, United Nations Development Programme (UNDP).

"Iniciativas del sector público a favor de los derechos culturales y la participación en la cultura en Bélgica (por Emilie Vidal)", Interarts Foundation, December 2007.

In from the margins: a contribution to the debate on culture and development in Europe, Council of Europe, the European Task Force on Culture and Development (1997), Council of Europe Publishing, Strasbourg.

"International Seminar on Diversity and Cultural Rights", Art Sem Fronteiras, Interarts Foundation and the Universal Forum of Cultures, 31 March-2 April 2004, São Paolo, Brazil.

"Local policies for cultural diversity", paper commissioned by the Division of Cultural Policies and Intercultural Dialogue of UNESCO to the Institute for Culture, Barcelona City Council, as Chair of the United Cities and Local Governments' Working Group on Culture, 2006.

National Minorities Cultural Autonomy Act, passed by the Act of 26 October 1993 (RT I 1993, 71, 1001), entered into force on 28 November 1993, Estonia.

Our creative diversity, World Commission on Culture and Development, UNESCO, 1995.

"Participatory arts", Arts Council of Ireland background discussion paper, June 2005.

"Policy guidelines", Civil Society Platform on Access to Culture, 2009.

"Preliminary draft protocol to the European Convention for the Protection of Human Rights and Fundamental Freedoms on the recognition of cultural rights", Institute for Interdisciplinary Ethical and Human Rights Studies, University of Fribourg, 1995.

"Report of a thematic study using transnational comparisons to analyse and identify cultural policies and programmes that contribute to preventing and reducing poverty and social exclusion, a report undertaken for the European Commission", Centre for Public Policy and Centre for Cultural Policy and Management of the University of Northumbria, 2004.

"Report of the International Seminar on the Right to Take Part in Cultural Life", Interarts Foundation and the Institute for Culture of Barcelona City Council, Barcelona, 15-16 November 2002.

"Right to Participate in Cultural Life", Report of the Pre-Dialogue for the International Dialogue on Cultural Rights and Human Development, April 2004, Amman, Jordan.

"Rights and commitments in the city. Introductory text", Interarts Foundation, 2002.

"Scotland's culture. Scottish Executive response on the Cultural Review", Scottish Executive 2006.

"Second periodical report on the European Charter for Regional or Minority Languages. Norway", March 2002, available at:

www.regjeringen.no/en/dep/kkd/Documents/rapporter_planer/rapporter/2002/European-charter-for-regional-or-minority-languages.html?id=420162.

"Social effects of culture; exploratory statistical evidence", report funded by the Canada Council for the Arts, the Department of Canadian Heritage and the Ontario Arts Council, March 2008.

"Strategic Planning of the Finnish Government", 2000.

"Summary report on the International Round Table on the Right to Take Part in Cultural Life", held on 11-13 February 2002, at the University of the Philippines, Quezon City.

"Taiteen ja kulttuurin saavutettavuus. Opetusministeriön toimenpideohjelma 2006-2010" [Accessibility of art and culture. Action plan of the ministry of education 2006-2010], Ministry of Education, Finland, 2006.

"The Banyan tree paradox. Culture and human rights activism", International Human Rights Internship Program (IHRIP), Institute of International Education, 2006.

"The impact of the arts: some research evidence", Arts Council England, 2004.

"Young people and culture", report of the EUROCITIES Working Group on Young People and Culture, 2009.

Annex

General comment No. 21 on the right of everyone to take part in cultural life (adopted by the United Nations Committee on Economic, Social and Cultural Rights of the Economic and Social Council in November 2009)

I. Introduction and basic premises

1. Cultural rights are an integral part of human rights and, like other rights, are universal, indivisible and interdependent. The full promotion of and respect for cultural rights is essential for the maintenance of human dignity and positive social interaction between individuals and communities in a diverse and multicultural world.

2. The right of everyone to take part in cultural life is closely related to the other cultural rights contained in article 15: the right to enjoy the benefits of scientific progress and its applications (art. 15, para. 1 (b)); the right of everyone to benefit from the protection of moral and material interests resulting from any scientific, literary or artistic production of which they are the author (art. 15, para. 1 (c)); and the right to freedom indispensable for scientific research and creative activity (art. 15, para. 3). The right of everyone to take part in cultural life is also intrinsically linked to the right to education (arts. 13 and 14), through which individuals and communities pass on their values, religion, customs, language and other cultural references, and which helps to foster an atmosphere of mutual understanding and respect for cultural values. The right to take part in cultural life is also interdependent on other rights enshrined in the Covenant, including the right of all peoples to self-determination (art. 1) and the right to an adequate standard of living (art. 11).

3. The right of everyone to take part in cultural life is also recognized in article 27, paragraph 1, of the Universal Declaration of Human Rights, which states that "everyone has the right freely to participate in the cultural life of the community". Other international instruments refer to the right to equal

participation in cultural activities;[56] the right to participate in all aspects of social and cultural life;[57] the right to participate fully in cultural and artistic life;[58] the right of access to and participation in cultural life;[59] and the right to take part on an equal basis with others in cultural life.[60] Instruments on civil and political rights,[61] on the rights of persons belonging to minorities to enjoy their own culture, to profess and practise their own religion, and to use their own language, in private and in public,[62] and to participate effectively in cultural life,[63] on the rights of indigenous peoples to their cultural institutions, ancestral lands, natural resources and traditional knowledge,[64] and on the right to development[65] also contain important provisions on this subject.

4. In the present general comment, the Committee addresses specifically the right of everyone under article 15 paragraph 1 (a), to take part in cultural life, in conjunction with paragraphs 2, 3 and 4, as they relate to culture, creative activity and the development of international contacts and cooperation in cultural fields, respectively. The right of everyone to benefit from the protection of moral and material interests resulting from any scientific, literary or artistic production of which they are the author, as provided for in article 15, paragraph 1 (c), was the subject of general comment No. 17 (2005).

5. The Committee has gained long experience on this subject through its consideration of reports and dialogue with States parties. In addition, it has twice organized a day of general discussion, once in 1992 and again in 2008, with representatives of international organizations and civil society with a view to preparing the present general comment.

56. International Convention on the Elimination of All Forms of Racial Discrimination, art. 5 (e) (vi).
57. Convention on the Elimination of All Forms of Discrimination against Women, art. 13 (c).
58. Convention on the Rights of the Child, art. 31, para. 2.
59. International Convention on the Protection of the Rights of All Migrant Workers and Members of Their Families, art. 43, para. 1 (g).
60. Convention on the Rights of Persons with Disabilities, art. 30, para. 1.
61. In particular the International Covenant on Civil and Political Rights, arts. 17, 18, 19, 21 and 22.
62. International Covenant on Civil and Political Rights, art. 27.
63. Declaration on the Rights of Persons Belonging to National or Ethnic, Religious and Linguistic Minorities, art. 2, paras. 1 and 2. See also Framework Convention for the Protection of National Minorities (Council of Europe, ETS No. 157), art. 15.
64. United Nations Declaration on the Rights of Indigenous Peoples, in particular arts. 5, 8, and 10-13 ff. See also ILO Convention No. 169 concerning Indigenous and Tribal Peoples in Independent Countries, in particular arts. 2, 5, 7, 8, and 13-15 ff.
65. Declaration on the Right to Development (General Assembly resolution 41/128), art. 1. In its general comment No. 4, paragraph 9, the Committee considers that rights cannot be viewed in isolation from other human rights contained in the two international Covenants and other applicable international instruments.

II. Normative content of article 15, paragraph 1 (a)

6. The right to take part in cultural life can be characterized as a freedom. In order for this right to be ensured, it requires from the State party both abstention (i.e., non-interference with the exercise of cultural practices and with access to cultural goods and services) and positive action (ensuring preconditions for participation, facilitation and promotion of cultural life, and access to and preservation of cultural goods).

7. The decision by a person whether or not to exercise the right to take part in cultural life individually, or in association with others, is a cultural choice and, as such, should be recognized, respected and protected on the basis of equality. This is especially important for all indigenous peoples, who have the right to the full enjoyment, as a collective or as individuals, of all human rights and fundamental freedoms as recognized in the Charter of the United Nations, the Universal Declaration of Human Rights and international human rights law, as well as the United Nations Declaration on the Rights of Indigenous Peoples.

A. Components of article 15, paragraph 1 (a)

8. The content or scope of the terms used in article 15, paragraph 1 (a), on the right of everyone to take part in cultural life, is to be understood as set out below:

"Everyone"

9. In its general comment No. 17 on the right to benefit from the protection of moral and material interests resulting from any scientific, literary or artistic production of which one is the author,[66] the Committee recognizes that the term "everyone" in the first line of article 15 may denote the individual or the collective; in other words, cultural rights may be exercised by a person (a) as an individual, (b) in association with others, or (c) within a community or group, as such.

---

66. See definition of "author" in general comment No. 17 (2005), paras. 7 and 8.

"Cultural life"

10. Various definitions of "culture" have been postulated in the past and others may arise in the future. All of them, however, refer to the multifaceted content implicit in the concept of culture.[67]

11. In the Committee's view, culture is a broad, inclusive concept encompassing all manifestations of human existence. The expression "cultural life" is an explicit reference to culture as a living process, historical, dynamic and evolving, with a past, a present and a future.

12. The concept of culture must be seen not as a series of isolated manifestations or hermetic compartments, but as an interactive process whereby individuals and communities, while preserving their specificities and purposes, give expression to the culture of humanity. This concept takes account of the individuality and otherness of culture as the creation and product of society.

13. The Committee considers that culture, for the purpose of implementing article 15 (1) (a), encompasses, inter alia, ways of life, language, oral and written literature, music and song, non-verbal communication, religion or belief systems, rites and ceremonies, sport and games, methods of production or technology, natural and man-made environments, food, clothing and shelter and the arts, customs and traditions through which individuals, groups of individuals and communities express their humanity and the meaning they give to their existence, and build their world view representing their encounter with the external forces affecting their lives. Culture shapes and mirrors the values of well-being and the economic, social and political life of individuals, groups of individuals and communities.

---

67. Culture is (a) "the set of distinctive spiritual, material, intellectual and emotional features of a society or a social group, [which] encompasses, in addition to art and literature, lifestyles, ways of living together, value systems, traditions and beliefs" (UNESCO Universal Declaration on Cultural Diversity, fifth preambular paragraph); (b) "in its very essence, a social phenomenon resulting from individuals joining and cooperating in creative activities [and] is not limited to access to works of art and the human rights, but is at one and the same time the acquisition of knowledge, the demand for a way of life and need to communicate" (UNESCO recommendation on participation by the people at large in cultural life and their contribution to it, 1976, the Nairobi recommendation, fifth preambular paragraph (a) and (c)); (c) "covers those values, beliefs, convictions, languages, knowledge and the arts, traditions, institutions and ways of life through which a person or a group expresses their humanity and meanings that they give to their existence and to their development" (Fribourg Declaration on Cultural Rights, art. 2 (a) (definitions); (d) "the sum total of the material and spiritual activities and products of a given social group which distinguishes it from other similar groups [and] a system of values and symbols as well as a set of practices that a specific cultural group reproduces over time and which provides individuals with the required signposts and meanings for behaviour and social relationships in everyday life". (Rodolfo Stavenhagen, "Cultural Rights: A social science perspective", in H. Niec (ed.), *Cultural Rights and Wrongs: A collection of essays in commemoration of the 50th anniversary of the Universal Declaration of Human Rights*, Paris and Leicester, UNESCO Publishing and Institute of Art and Law).

"To participate" or "to take part"

14. The terms "to participate" and "to take part" have the same meaning and are used interchangeably in other international and regional instruments.

15. There are, among others, three interrelated main components of the right to participate or take part in cultural life: (a) participation in, (b) access to, and (c) contribution to cultural life.

    (a). *Participation* covers in particular the right of everyone – alone, or in association with others or as a community – to act freely, to choose his or her own identity, to identify or not with one or several communities or to change that choice, to take part in the political life of society, to engage in one's own cultural practices and to express oneself in the language of one's choice. Everyone also has the right to seek and develop cultural knowledge and expressions and to share them with others, as well as to act creatively and take part in creative activity;

    (b). *Access* covers in particular the right of everyone – alone, in association with others or as a community – to know and understand his or her own culture and that of others through education and information, and to receive quality education and training with due regard for cultural identity. Everyone has also the right to learn about forms of expression and dissemination through any technical medium of information or communication, to follow a way of life associated with the use of cultural goods and resources such as land, water,[68] biodiversity, language or specific institutions, and to benefit from the cultural heritage and the creation of other individuals and communities;

    (c). *Contribution to cultural life* refers to the right of everyone to be involved in creating the spiritual, material, intellectual and emotional expressions of the community. This is supported by the right to take part in the development of the community to which a person belongs, and in the definition, elaboration and implementation of policies and decisions that have an impact on the exercise of a person's cultural rights.[69]

---

68. General comment No. 15 (2002), paras. 6 and 11.
69. UNESCO Universal Declaration on Cultural Diversity, art. 5. See also Fribourg Declaration on Cultural Rights, art. 7.

B. Elements of the right to take part in cultural life

16. The following are necessary conditions for the full realization of the right of everyone to take part in cultural life on the basis of equality and non-discrimination.

(a). *Availability* is the presence of cultural goods and services that are open for everyone to enjoy and benefit from, including libraries, museums, theatres, cinemas and sports stadiums; literature, including folklore, and the arts in all forms; the shared open spaces essential to cultural interaction, such as parks, squares, avenues and streets; nature's gifts, such as seas, lakes, rivers, mountains, forests and nature reserves, including the flora and fauna found there, which give nations their character and biodiversity; intangible cultural goods, such as languages, customs, traditions, beliefs, knowledge and history, as well as values, which make up identity and contribute to the cultural diversity of individuals and communities. Of all the cultural goods, one of special value is the productive intercultural kinship that arises where diverse groups, minorities and communities can freely share the same territory;

(b). *Accessibility* consists of effective and concrete opportunities for individuals and communities to enjoy culture fully, within physical and financial reach for all in both urban and rural areas, without discrimination.[70] It is essential, in this regard, that access for older persons and persons with disabilities, as well as for those who live in poverty, is provided and facilitated. Accessibility also includes the right of everyone to seek, receive and share information on all manifestations of culture in the language of the person's choice, and the access of communities to means of expressions and dissemination.

(c). *Acceptability* entails that the laws, policies, strategies, programmes and measures adopted by the State party for the enjoyment of cultural rights should be formulated and implemented in such a way as to be acceptable to the individuals and communities involved. In this regard, consultations should be held with the individuals and communities concerned in order to ensure that the measures to protect cultural diversity are acceptable to them;

---

70. See general comment No. 20 (2009).

(d). *Adaptability* refers to the flexibility and relevance of strategies, policies, programmes and measures adopted by the State party in any area of cultural life, which must be respectful of the cultural diversity of individuals and communities;

(e). *Appropriateness* refers to the realization of a specific human right in a way that is pertinent and suitable to a given cultural modality or context, that is, respectful of the culture and cultural rights of individuals and communities, including minorities and indigenous peoples.[71] The Committee has in many instances referred to the notion of cultural appropriateness (or cultural acceptability or adequacy) in past general comments, in relation in particular to the rights to food, health, water, housing and education. The way in which rights are implemented may also have an impact on cultural life and cultural diversity. The Committee wishes to stress in this regard the need to take into account, as far as possible, cultural values attached to, inter alia, food and food consumption, the use of water, the way health and education services are provided and the way housing is designed and constructed.

C. Limitations to the right to take part in cultural life

17. The right of everyone to take part in cultural life is closely linked to the enjoyment of other rights recognized in the international human rights instruments. Consequently, States parties have a duty to implement their obligations under article 15, paragraph 1 (a), together with their obligations under other provisions of the Covenant and international instruments, in order to promote and protect the entire range of human rights guaranteed under international law.

18. The Committee wishes to recall that, while account must be taken of national and regional particularities and various historical, cultural and religious backgrounds, it is the duty of States, regardless of their political, economic or cultural systems, to promote and protect all human rights and fundamental freedoms.[72] Thus, no one may invoke cultural diversity to infringe upon human rights guaranteed by international law, nor to limit their scope.[73]

---

71. Fribourg Declaration on Cultural Rights, art. 1 (e).
72. Vienna Declaration and Programme of Action, para. 5.
73. Universal Declaration on Cultural Diversity, art. 4.

19. Applying limitations to the right of everyone to take part in cultural life may be necessary in certain circumstances, in particular in the case of negative practices, including those attributed to customs and traditions, that infringe upon other human rights. Such limitations must pursue a legitimate aim, be compatible with the nature of this right and be strictly necessary for the promotion of general welfare in a democratic society, in accordance with article 4 of the Covenant. Any limitations must therefore be proportionate, meaning that the least restrictive measures must be taken when several types of limitations may be imposed. The Committee also wishes to stress the need to take into consideration existing international human rights standards on limitations that can or cannot be legitimately imposed on rights that are intrinsically linked to the right to take part in cultural life, such as the rights to privacy, to freedom of thought, conscience and religion, to freedom of opinion and expression, to peaceful assembly and to freedom of association.

20. Article 15, paragraph 1 (a) may not be interpreted as implying for any State, group or person any right to engage in any activity or perform any act aimed at the destruction of any of the rights and freedoms recognized in the Covenant or at their limitation to a greater extent than is provided for therein.[74]

D. Special topics of broad application

Non-discrimination and equal treatment

21. Article 2, paragraph 2, and article 3 of the Covenant prohibit any discrimination in the exercise of the right of everyone to take part in cultural life on the grounds of race, colour, sex, language, religion, political or other opinion, national or social origin, property, birth or other status.[75]

22. In particular, no one shall be discriminated against because he or she chooses to belong, or not to belong, to a given cultural community or group, or to practise or not to practise a particular cultural activity. Likewise, no one shall be excluded from access to cultural practices, goods and services.

---

74. International Covenant on Economic, Social and Cultural Rights, art. 5, para. 1.
75. See general comment No. 20 (2009).

23. The Committee emphasizes that the elimination of all forms of discrimination in order to guarantee the exercise of the right of everyone to take part in cultural life can, in many cases, be achieved with limited resources[76] by the adoption, amendment or repeal of legislation, or through publicity and information. In particular, a first and important step towards the elimination of discrimination, whether direct or indirect, is for States to recognize the existence of diverse cultural identities of individuals and communities on their territories. The Committee also refers States parties to its general comment No. 3 (1990), paragraph 12, on the nature of States parties' obligations, which establishes that, even in times of severe resource constraints, the most disadvantaged and marginalized individuals and groups can and indeed must be protected by the adoption of relatively low-cost targeted programmes.

24. The adoption of temporary special measures with the sole purpose of achieving de facto equality does not constitute discrimination, provided that such measures do not perpetuate unequal protection or form a separate system of protection for certain individuals or groups of individuals, and that they are discontinued when the objectives for which they were taken have been achieved.

E. Persons and communities requiring special protection

1. Women

25. Ensuring the equal right of men and women to the enjoyment of economic, social and cultural rights is a mandatory and immediate obligation of States parties.[77] Implementing article 3 of the Covenant, in relation to article 15, paragraph 1 (a), requires, inter alia, the elimination of institutional and legal obstacles as well as those based on negative practices, including those attributed to customs and traditions, that prevent women from participating fully in cultural life, science education and scientific research.[78]

---

76. See general comment No. 3 (1990); statement by the Committee: an evaluation of the obligation to take steps to the "maximum of available resources" under an optional protocol to the Covenant (E/C.12/2007/1).

77. General comment No. 16 (2005), para. 16.

78. Ibid., para. 31.

2. Children

26. Children play a fundamental role as the bearers and transmitters of cultural values from generation to generation. States parties should take all the steps necessary to stimulate and develop children's full potential in the area of cultural life, with due regard for the rights and responsibilities of their parents or guardians. In particular, when taking into consideration their obligations under the Covenant and other human rights instruments on the right to education, including with regard to the aims of education,[79] States should recall that the fundamental aim of educational development is the transmission and enrichment of common cultural and moral values in which the individual and society find their identity and worth.[80] Thus, education must be culturally appropriate, include human rights education, enable children to develop their personality and cultural identity and to learn and understand cultural values and practices of the communities to which they belong, as well as those of other communities and societies.

27. The Committee wishes to recall in this regard that educational programmes of States parties should respect the cultural specificities of national or ethnic, linguistic and religious minorities as well as indigenous peoples, and incorporate in those programmes their history, knowledge and technologies, as well as their social, economic and cultural values and aspirations. Such programmes should be included in school curricula for all, not only for minorities and indigenous peoples. States parties should adopt measures and spare no effort to ensure that educational programmes for minorities and indigenous groups are conducted on or in their own language, taking into consideration the wishes expressed by communities and in the international human rights standards in this area.[81] Educational programmes should also transmit the necessary knowledge to enable everyone to participate fully and on an equal footing in their own and in national communities.

---

79. In particular articles 28 and 29 of the Convention on the Rights of the Child.

80. World Declaration on Education for All: Meeting Basic Learning Needs, arts. I-3.

81. In particular the Declaration on the Rights of Persons Belonging to National or Ethnic, Religious and Linguistic Minorities, the Declaration on the Rights of Indigenous Peoples and the International Labour Organization Convention concerning Indigenous and Tribal Peoples in Independent Countries (Convention No. 169).

3. Older persons

28. The Committee is of the view that States parties to the Covenant are obligated to pay particular attention to the promotion and protection of the cultural rights of older persons. The Committee emphasizes the important role that older persons continue to play in most societies by reason of their creative, artistic and intellectual abilities, and as the transmitters of information, knowledge, traditions and cultural values. Consequently, the Committee attaches particular importance to the message contained in recommendations 44 and 48 of the Vienna International Plan of Action on Aging, calling for the development of programmes featuring older persons as teachers and transmitters of knowledge, culture and spiritual values, and encouraging Governments and international organizations to support programmes aimed at providing older persons with easier physical access to cultural institutions (such as museums, theatres, concert halls and cinemas).[82]

29. The Committee therefore urges States parties to take account of the recommendations contained in the United Nations Principles for Older Persons, and in particular of principle 7, that older persons should remain integrated in society, participate actively in the formulation and implementation of policies that directly affect their well-being and share their knowledge and skills with younger generations; and principle 16, that older persons should have access to the educational, cultural, spiritual and recreational resources of society.[83]

4. Persons with disabilities

30. Paragraph 17 of the Standard Rules on the Equalization of Opportunities for Persons with Disabilities provides that States should ensure that persons with disabilities have the opportunity to utilize their creative, artistic and intellectual potential, not only for their own benefit, but also for the enrichment of their community, be they in urban or rural areas, and that States should promote accessibility to and availability of places for cultural performances and services.[84]

---

82. General comment No. 6 (1995), paras. 38 and 40.
83. General comment No. 6 (1995), para. 39.
84. General Assembly resolution 48/96, annex.

31. In order to facilitate participation of persons with disabilities in cultural life, States parties should, inter alia, recognize the right of these persons to have access to cultural material, television programmes, films, theatre and other cultural activities, in accessible forms; to have access to places where cultural performances or services are offered, such as theatres, museums, cinemas, libraries and tourist services and, to the extent possible, to monuments and places of national cultural importance; to the recognition of their specific cultural and linguistic identity, including sign language and the culture of the deaf; and to the encouragement and promotion of their participation, to the extent possible, in recreational, leisure and sporting activities.[85]

5. Minorities

32. In the Committee's view, article 15, paragraph 1 (a) of the Covenant also includes the right of minorities and of persons belonging to minorities to take part in the cultural life of society, and also to conserve, promote and develop their own culture.[86] This right entails the obligation of States parties to recognize, respect and protect minority cultures as an essential component of the identity of the States themselves. Consequently, minorities have the right to their cultural diversity, traditions, customs, religion, forms of education, languages, communication media (press, radio, television, Internet) and other manifestations of their cultural identity and membership.

33. Minorities, as well as persons belonging to minorities, have the right not only to their own identity but also to development in all areas of cultural life. Any programme intended to promote the constructive integration of minorities and persons belonging to minorities into the society of a State party should thus be based on inclusion, participation and non-discrimination, with a view to preserving the distinctive character of minority cultures.

---

85. Convention on the Rights of Persons with Disabilities, art. 30.
86. International Covenant on Civil and Political Rights, art. 27; Declaration on the Rights of Persons Belonging to National or Ethnic, Religious and Linguistic Minorities, para. 1 (1).

6. Migrants

34. States parties should pay particular attention to the protection of the cultural identities of migrants, as well as their language, religion and folklore, and of their right to hold cultural, artistic and intercultural events. States parties should not prevent migrants from maintaining their cultural links with their countries of origin.[87]

35. As education is intrinsically related to culture, the Committee recommends that States parties adopt appropriate measures to enable the children of migrants to attend, on a basis of equal treatment, State-run educational institution and programmes.

7. Indigenous peoples

36. States parties should take measures to guarantee that the exercise of the right to take part in cultural life takes due account of the values of cultural life, which may be strongly communal or which can only be expressed and enjoyed as a community by indigenous peoples.[88] The strong communal dimension of indigenous peoples' cultural life is indispensable to their existence, well-being and full development, and includes the right to the lands, territories and resources which they have traditionally owned, occupied or otherwise used or acquired.[89] Indigenous peoples' cultural values and rights associated with their ancestral lands and their relationship with nature should be regarded with respect and protected, in order to prevent the degradation of their particular way of life, including their means of subsistence, the loss of their natural resources and, ultimately, their cultural identity.[90] States parties must therefore take measures to recognize and protect the rights of indigenous peoples to own, develop, control and use their communal lands, territories and resources, and, where they have been otherwise inhabited or used without their free and informed consent, take steps to return these lands and territories.

87. International Convention on the Protection of the Rights of All Migrant Workers and Members of Their Families, art. 31.
88. See Declaration on the Rights of Indigenous Peoples, art. 1. See also ILO Convention concerning Indigenous and Tribal Peoples in Independent Countries (Convention No. 169), art. 1, para. 2.
89. United Nations Declaration on the Rights of Indigenous Peoples, art. 26 (a).
90. Convention No. 169, arts. 13-16. See also the United Nations Declaration on the Rights of Indigenous Peoples, arts. 20 and 33.

37. Indigenous peoples have the right to act collectively to ensure respect for their right to maintain, control, protect and develop their cultural heritage, traditional knowledge and traditional cultural expressions, as well as the manifestations of their sciences, technologies and cultures, including human and genetic resources, seeds, medicines, knowledge of the properties of fauna and flora, oral traditions, literature, designs, sports and traditional games, and visual and performing arts.[91] States parties should respect the principle of free, prior and informed consent of indigenous peoples in all matters covered by their specific rights.[92]

8. Persons living in poverty

38. The Committee considers that every person or group of persons is endowed with a cultural richness inherent in their humanity and therefore can make, and continues to make, a significant contribution to the development of culture. Nevertheless, it must be borne in mind that, in practice, poverty seriously restricts the ability of a person or a group of persons to exercise the right to take part in, gain access and contribute to, on equal terms, all spheres of cultural life, and more importantly, seriously affects their hopes for the future and their ability to enjoy effectively their own culture. The common underlying theme in the experience of persons living in poverty is a sense of powerlessness that is often a consequence of their situation. Awareness of their human rights, and particularly the right of every person to take part in cultural life, can significantly empower persons or groups of persons living in poverty.[93]

39. Culture as a social product must be brought within the reach of all, on the basis of equality, non-discrimination and participation. Therefore, in implementing the legal obligations enshrined in article 15, paragraph 1 (a), of the Covenant, States parties must adopt, without delay, concrete measures to ensure adequate protection and the full exercise of the right of persons living in poverty and their communities to enjoy and take part in cultural life. In this respect, the Committee refers States parties to its statement on poverty and the International Covenant on Economic, Social and Cultural Rights.[94]

---

91. ILO Convention No. 169, arts. 5 and 31. See also the United Nations Declaration on the Rights of Indigenous Peoples, arts. 11-13.
92. ILO Convention No. 169, art. 6 (a). See also the United Nations Declaration on the Rights of Indigenous Peoples, art. 19.
93. See E/C.12/2001/10, para. 5.
94. Ibid., para. 14.

F. Cultural diversity and the right to take part in cultural life

40. The protection of cultural diversity is an ethical imperative, inseparable from respect for human dignity. It implies a commitment to human rights and fundamental freedoms, and requires the full implementation of cultural rights, including the right to take part in cultural life.[95]

41. Cultures have no fixed borders. The phenomena of migration, integration, assimilation and globalization have brought cultures, groups and individuals into closer contact than ever before, at a time when each of them is striving to keep their own identity.

42. Given that globalization has positive and negative effects, States parties must take appropriate steps to avoid its adverse consequences on the right to take part in cultural life, particularly for the most disadvantaged and marginalized individuals and groups, such as persons living in poverty. Far from having produced a single world culture, globalization has demonstrated that the concept of culture implies the coexistence of different cultures.

43. States parties should also bear in mind that cultural activities, goods and services have economic and cultural dimensions, conveying identity, values and meanings. They must not be treated as having solely a commercial value.[96] In particular, bearing in mind article 15 (2) of the Covenant, States parties should adopt measures to protect and promote the diversity of cultural expressions,[97] and enable all cultures to express themselves and make themselves known.[98] In this respect, due regard should be paid to human rights standards, including the right to information and expression, and to the need to protect the free flow of ideas by word and image. The measures may also aim at preventing the signs, symbols and expressions of a particular culture from being taken out of context for the sole purpose of marketing or exploitation by the mass media.

---

95. See the Universal Declaration on Cultural Diversity, arts. 4 and 5.
96. UNESCO Convention on the Protection and Promotion of the Diversity of Cultural Expressions, preamble, para. 18. See also the Universal Declaration on Cultural Diversity, art. 8.
97. UNESCO Convention on the Protection and Promotion of the Diversity of Cultural Expressions, art. IV-5.
98. See the Universal Declaration on Cultural Diversity, art. 6.

III. States parties' obligations

A. General legal obligations

44. The Covenant imposes on States parties the immediate obligation to guarantee that the right set out in article 15, paragraph 1 (a), is exercised without discrimination, to recognize cultural practices and to refrain from interfering in their enjoyment and development.[99]

45. While the Covenant provides for the "progressive" realization of the rights set out in its provisions and recognizes the problems arising from limited resources, it imposes on States parties the specific and continuing obligation to take deliberate and concrete measures aimed at the full implementation of the right of everyone to take part in cultural life.[100]

46. As in the case of the other rights set out in the Covenant, regressive measures taken in relation to the right of everyone to take part in cultural life are not permitted. Consequently, if any such measure is taken deliberately, the State party has to prove that it was taken after careful consideration of all alternatives and that the measure in question is justified, bearing in mind the complete set of rights recognized in the Covenant.[101]

47. Given the interrelationship between the rights set out in article 15 of the Covenant (see paragraph 2 above), the full realization of the right of everyone to take part in cultural life also requires the adoption of steps necessary for the conservation, development and dissemination of science and culture, as well as steps to ensure respect for the freedom indispensable to scientific research and creative activity, in accordance with paragraphs 2 and 3, respectively, of article 15.[102]

---

99. See general comment No. 20 (2009).

100. See general comments No. 3 (1990), para. 9, No. 13 (1999), para. 44, No. 14 (2000), para. 31, No. 17 (2005), para. 26 and No. 18 (2005), para. 20. See also the Limburg Principles on the Implementation of the International Covenant on Economic, Social and Cultural Rights, para. 21.

101. See general comments No. 3 (1990), para. 9, No. 13 (1999), para. 45, No. 14 (2000), para. 32, No. 17 (2005), para. 27 and No. 18 (2005), para. 21.

102. See general comments No. 13 (1999), paras. 46 and 47, No. 14 (2000), para. 33, No. 17 (2005), para. 28 and No. 18 (2005), para. 22.

B. Specific legal obligations

48. The right of everyone to take part in cultural life, like the other rights enshrined in the Covenant, imposes three types or levels of obligations on States parties: (a) the obligation to respect; (b) the obligation to protect; and (c) the obligation to fulfil. The obligation to respect requires States parties to refrain from interfering, directly or indirectly, with the enjoyment of the right to take part in cultural life. The obligation to protect requires States parties to take steps to prevent third parties from interfering in the right to take part in cultural life. Lastly, the obligation to fulfil requires States parties to take appropriate legislative, administrative, judicial, budgetary, promotional and other measures aimed at the full realization of the right enshrined in article 15, paragraph 1 (a), of the Covenant.[103]

49. The obligation to respect includes the adoption of specific measures aimed at achieving respect for the right of everyone, individually or in association with others or within a community or group:

   (a). To freely choose their own cultural identity, to belong or not to belong to a community, and have their choice respected;

   This includes the right not to be subjected to any form of discrimination based on cultural identity, exclusion or forced assimilation,[104] and the right of all persons to express their cultural identity freely and to exercise their cultural practices and way of life. States parties should consequently ensure that their legislation does not impair the enjoyment of these rights through direct or indirect discrimination.

   (b). To enjoy freedom of opinion, freedom of expression in the language or languages of their choice, and the right to seek, receive and impart information and ideas of all kinds and forms including art forms, regardless of frontiers of any kind;

   This implies the right of all persons to have access to, and to participate in, varied information exchanges, and to have access to cultural goods and services, understood as vectors of identity, values and meaning.[105]

---

103. See general comments No. 13 (1990), paras. 46 and 47, No. 14 (2000), para. 33, No. 17 (2005), para. 28 and No. 18 (2005), para. 22. See also the Limburg Principles on the Implementation of the International Covenant on Economic, Social and Cultural Rights, para. 6.
104. International Convention on the Protection of the Rights of All Migrant Workers and Members of Their Families, art. 31.
105. Universal Declaration on Cultural Diversity, para. 8.

(c). To enjoy the freedom to create, individually, in association with others, or within a community or group, which implies that States parties must abolish censorship of cultural activities in the arts and other forms of expression, if any;

This obligation is closely related to the duty of States parties, under article 15, paragraph 3, "to respect the freedom indispensable for scientific research and creative activity".

(d). To have access to their own cultural and linguistic heritage and to that of others;

In particular, States must respect free access by minorities to their own culture, heritage and other forms of expression, as well as the free exercise of their cultural identity and practices. This includes the right to be taught about one's own culture as well as those of others.[106] States parties must also respect the rights of indigenous peoples to their culture and heritage and to maintain and strengthen their spiritual relationship with their ancestral lands and other natural resources traditionally owned, occupied or used by them, and indispensable to their cultural life.

(e). To take part freely in an active and informed way, and without discrimination, in any important decision-making process that may have an impact on his or her way of life and on his or her rights under article 15, paragraph 1 (a).

50. In many instances, the obligations to respect and to protect freedoms, cultural heritage and diversity are interconnected. Consequently, the obligation to protect is to be understood as requiring States to take measures to prevent third parties from interfering in the exercise of rights listed in paragraph 49 above. In addition, States parties are obliged to:

(a). Respect and protect cultural heritage in all its forms, in times of war and peace, and natural disasters;

Cultural heritage must be preserved, developed, enriched and transmitted to future generations as a record of human experience and aspirations, in order to encourage creativity in all its diversity and to inspire a genuine dialogue between cultures. Such obligations include the care, preservation and restoration of historical sites, monuments, works of art and literary works, among others.[107]

106. Fribourg Declaration on Cultural Rights, arts. 6 (b) and 7 (b).
107. Universal Declaration on Cultural Diversity, art. 7.

(b). Respect and protect cultural heritage of all groups and communities, in particular the most disadvantaged and marginalized individuals and groups, in economic development and environmental policies and programmes;

Particular attention should be paid to the adverse consequences of globalization, undue privatization of goods and services, and deregulation on the right to participate in cultural life.

(c). Respect and protect the cultural productions of indigenous peoples, including their traditional knowledge, natural medicines, folklore, rituals and other forms of expression;

This includes protection from illegal or unjust exploitation of their lands, territories and resources by State entities or private or transnational enterprises and corporations.

(d). Promulgate and enforce legislation to prohibit discrimination based on cultural identity, as well as advocacy of national, racial or religious hatred that constitutes incitement to discrimination, hostility or violence, taking into consideration articles 19 and 20 of the International Covenant on Civil and Political Rights and article 4 of the International Convention on the Elimination of All Forms of Racial Discrimination.

51. The obligation to fulfil can be subdivided into the obligations to facilitate, promote and provide.

52. States parties are under an obligation to facilitate the right of everyone to take part in cultural life by taking a wide range of positive measures, including financial measures, that would contribute to the realization of this right, such as:

(a). Adopting policies for the protection and promotion of cultural diversity, and facilitating access to a rich and diversified range of cultural expressions, including through, inter alia, measures aimed at establishing and supporting public institutions and the cultural infrastructure necessary for the implementation of such policies; and measures aimed at enhancing diversity through public broadcasting in regional and minority languages;

(b). Adopting policies enabling persons belonging to diverse cultural communities to engage freely and without discrimination in their own cultural practices and those of others, and to choose freely their way of life;

(c). Promoting the exercise of the right of association for cultural and linguistic minorities for the development of their cultural and linguistic rights;

(d). Granting assistance, financial or other, to artists, public and private organizations, including science academies, cultural associations, trade unions and other individuals and institutions engaged in scientific and creative activities;

(e). Encouraging scientists, artists and others to take part in international scientific and cultural research activities, such as symposiums, conferences, seminars and workshops;

(f). Taking appropriate measures or programmes to support minorities or other communities, including migrant communities, in their efforts to preserve their culture;

(g). Taking appropriate measures to remedy structural forms of discrimination so as to ensure that the underrepresentation of persons from certain communities in public life does not adversely affect their right to take part in cultural life;

(h). Taking appropriate measures to create conditions conducive to a constructive intercultural relationship between individuals and groups based on mutual respect, understanding and tolerance;

(i). Taking appropriate measures to conduct public campaigns through the media, educational institutions and other available channels, with a view to eliminating any form of prejudice against individuals or communities, based on their cultural identity.

53. The obligation to promote requires States parties to take effective steps to ensure that there is appropriate education and public awareness concerning the right to take part in cultural life, particularly in rural and deprived urban areas, or in relation to the specific situation of, inter alia, minorities and indigenous peoples. This includes education and awareness-raising on the need to respect cultural heritage and cultural diversity.

54. The obligation to fulfil requires that States parties must provide all that is necessary for fulfilment of the right to take part in cultural life when individuals or communities are unable, for reasons outside their control, to realize this right for themselves with the means at their disposal. This level of obligation includes, for example:

(a). The enactment of appropriate legislation and the establishment of effective mechanisms allowing persons, individually, in association with others, or within a community or group, to participate effectively in decision-making processes, to claim protection of their right to take part in cultural life, and to claim and receive compensation if their rights have been violated;

(b). Programmes aimed at preserving and restoring cultural heritage;

(c). The inclusion of cultural education at every level in school curricula, including history, literature, music and the history of other cultures, in consultation with all concerned;

(d). Guaranteed access for all, without discrimination on grounds of financial or any other status, to museums, libraries, cinemas and theatres and to cultural activities, services and events.

C. Core obligations

55. In its general comment No. 3 (1990), the Committee stressed that States parties have a minimum core obligation to ensure the satisfaction of, at the very least, minimum essential levels of each of the rights set out in the Covenant. Thus, in accordance with the Covenant and other international instruments dealing with human rights and the protection of cultural diversity, the Committee considers that article 15, paragraph 1 (a), of the Covenant entails at least the obligation to create and promote an environment within which a person individually, or in association with others, or within a community or group, can participate in the culture of their choice, which includes the following core obligations applicable with immediate effect:

(a). To take legislative and any other necessary steps to guarantee non-discrimination and gender equality in the enjoyment of the right of everyone to take part in cultural life;

(b). To respect the right of everyone to identify or not identify themselves with one or more communities, and the right to change their choice;

(c). To respect and protect the right of everyone to engage in their own cultural practices, while respecting human rights which entails, in particular, respecting freedom of thought, belief and religion; freedom of opinion and expression; a person's right to use the language of his or her choice; freedom of association and peaceful assembly; and freedom to choose and set up educational establishments;

(d). To eliminate any barriers or obstacles that inhibit or restrict a person's access to the person's own culture or to other cultures, without discrimination and without consideration for frontiers of any kind;

(e). To allow and encourage the participation of persons belonging to minority groups, indigenous peoples or to other communities in the design and implementation of laws and policies that affect them. In particular, States parties should obtain their free and informed prior consent when the preservation of their cultural resources, especially those associated with their way of life and cultural expression, are at risk.

D. International obligations

56. In its general comment No. 3 (1990), the Committee draws attention to the obligation of States parties to take steps, individually and through international assistance and cooperation, especially through economic and technical cooperation, with a view to achieving the full realization of the rights recognized in the Covenant. In the spirit of Article 56 of the Charter of the United Nations, as well as specific provisions of the International Covenant on Economic, Social and Cultural Rights (art. 2, para. 1, and arts. 15 and 23), States parties should recognize and promote the essential role of international cooperation in the achievement of the rights recognized in the Covenant, including the right of everyone to take part in cultural life, and should fulfil their commitment to take joint and separate action to that effect.

57. States parties should, through international agreements where appropriate, ensure that the realization of the right of everyone to take part in cultural life receives due attention.[108]

58. The Committee recalls that international cooperation for development and thus for the realization of economic, social and cultural rights, including the right to take part in cultural life, is an obligation of States parties, especially of those States that are in a position to provide assistance. This obligation is in accordance with Articles 55 and 56 of the Charter of the United Nations, as well as articles 2, paragraph 1, and articles 15 and 23 of the Covenant.[109]

---

108. See general comment No. 18 (2005), para. 29.
109. General comment No. 3 (1990), para. 14. See also general comment No. 18 (2005), para. 37.

59. In negotiations with international financial institutions and in concluding bilateral agreements, States parties should ensure that the enjoyment of the right enshrined in article 15, paragraph 1 (a), of the Covenant is not impaired. For example, the strategies, programmes and policies adopted by States parties under structural adjustment programmes should not interfere with their core obligations in relation to the right of everyone, especially the most disadvantaged and marginalized individuals and groups, to take part in cultural life.[110]

IV. Violations

60. To demonstrate compliance with their general and specific obligations, States parties must show that they have taken appropriate measures to ensure the respect for and protection of cultural freedoms, as well as the necessary steps towards the full realization of the right to take part in cultural life within their maximum available resources. States parties must also show that they have guaranteed that the right is enjoyed equally and without discrimination, by men and women.

61. In assessing whether States parties have complied with obligations to take action, the Committee looks at whether implementation is reasonable or proportionate with respect to the attainment of the relevant rights, complies with human rights and democratic principles, and whether it is subject to an adequate framework of monitoring and accountability.

62. Violations can occur through the direct action of a State party or of other entities or institutions that are insufficiently regulated by the State party, including, in particular, those in the private sector. Many violations of the right to take part in cultural life occur when States parties prevent access to cultural life, practices, goods and services by individuals or communities.

63. Violations of article 15, paragraph 1 (a), also occur through the omission or failure of a State party to take the necessary measures to comply with its legal obligations under this provision. Violations through omission include the failure to take appropriate steps to achieve the full realization of the right of everyone to take part in cultural life, and the failure to enforce relevant laws or to provide administrative, judicial or other appropriate remedies to enable people to exercise in full the right to take part in cultural life.

---

110. See general comment No. 18 (2005), para. 30.

64. A violation also occurs when a State party fails to take steps to combat practices harmful to the well-being of a person or group of persons. These harmful practices, including those attributed to customs and traditions, such as female genital mutilation and allegations of the practice of witchcraft, are barriers to the full exercise by the affected persons of the right enshrined in article 15, paragraph 1 (a).

65. Any deliberately retrogressive measures in relation to the right to take part in cultural life would require the most careful consideration and need to be fully justified by reference to the totality of the rights provided for in the Covenant and in the context of the full use of the maximum available resources.

V. Implementation at the national level

A. Legislation, strategies and policies

66. While States parties have a wide margin of discretion in selecting the steps they consider most appropriate for the full realization of the right, they must immediately take those steps intended to guarantee access by everyone, without discrimination, to cultural life.

67. States parties must take the necessary steps without delay to guarantee immediately at least the minimum content of the core obligations (see paragraph 56 above). Many of these steps, such as those intended to guarantee non-discrimination de jure, do not necessarily require financial resources. While there may be other steps that require resources, these steps are nevertheless essential to ensure the implementation of that minimum content. Such steps are not static, and States parties are obliged to advance progressively towards the full realization of the rights recognized in the Covenant and, as far as the present general comment is concerned, of the right enshrined in article 15, paragraph 1 (a).

68. The Committee encourages States parties to make the greatest possible use of the valuable cultural resources that every society possesses and to bring them within the reach of everyone, paying particular attention to the most disadvantaged and marginalized individuals and groups, in order to ensure that everyone has effective access to cultural life.

69. The Committee emphasizes that inclusive cultural empowerment derived from the right of everyone to take part in cultural life is a tool for reducing the disparities so that everyone can enjoy, on an equal footing, the values of his or her own culture within a democratic society.

70. States parties, in implementing the right enshrined in article 15, paragraph 1 (a), of the Covenant, should go beyond the material aspects of culture (such as museums, libraries, theatres, cinemas, monuments and heritage sites) and adopt policies, programmes and proactive measures that also promote effective access by all to intangible cultural goods (such as language, knowledge and traditions).

B. Indicators and benchmarks

71. In their national strategies and policies, States parties should identify appropriate indicators and benchmarks, including disaggregated statistics and time frames that allow them to monitor effectively the implementation of the right of everyone to take part in cultural life, and also to assess progress towards the full realization of this right.

C. Remedies and accountability

72. The strategies and policies adopted by States parties should provide for the establishment of effective mechanisms and institutions, where these do not exist, to investigate and examine alleged infringements of article 15, paragraph 1 (a), identify responsibilities, publicize the results and offer the necessary administrative, judicial or other remedies to compensate victims.

VI. Obligations of actors other than States

73. While compliance with the Covenant is mainly the responsibility of States parties, all members of civil society – individuals, groups, communities, minorities, indigenous peoples, religious bodies, private organizations, business and civil society in general – also have responsibilities in relation to the effective implementation of the right of everyone to take part in cultural life. States parties should

regulate the responsibility incumbent upon the corporate sector and other non-State actors with regard to the respect for this right.

74. Communities and cultural associations play a fundamental role in the promotion of the right of everyone to take part in cultural life at the local and national levels, and in cooperating with States parties in the implementation of their obligations under article 15, paragraph 1 (a).

75. The Committee notes that, as members of international organizations such as United Nations Educational, Scientific and Cultural Organization (UNESCO), the World Intellectual Property Organization (WIPO), the International Labour Organization (ILO), the Food and Agriculture Organization of the United Nations (FAO), the World Health Organization (WHO) and the World Trade Organization (WTO), States parties have an obligation to adopt whatever measures they can to ensure that the policies and decisions of those organizations in the field of culture and related areas are in conformity with their obligations under the Covenant, in particular the obligations contained in article 15 article 2, paragraph 1, and articles 22 and 23, concerning international assistance and cooperation.

76. United Nations organs and specialized agencies, should, within their fields of competence and in accordance with articles 22 and 23 of the Covenant, adopt international measures likely to contribute to the progressive implementation of article 15, paragraph 1 (a). In particular, UNESCO, WIPO, ILO, FAO, WHO and other relevant agencies, funds and programmes of the United Nations are called upon to intensify their efforts to take into account human rights principles and obligations in their work concerning the right of everyone to take part in cultural life, in cooperation with the Office of the United Nations High Commissioner for Human Rights.

Sales agents for publications of the Council of Europe
Agents de vente des publications du Conseil de l'Europe

BELGIUM/BELGIQUE
La Librairie Européenne -
The European Bookshop
Rue de l'Orme, 1
BE-1040 BRUXELLES
Tel.: +32 (0)2 231 04 35
Fax: +32 (0)2 735 08 60
E-mail: order@libeurop.be
http://www.libeurop.be

Jean De Lannoy/DL Services
Avenue du Roi 202 Koningslaan
BE-1190 BRUXELLES
Tel.: +32 (0)2 538 43 08
Fax: +32 (0)2 538 08 41
E-mail: jean.de.lannoy@dl-servi.com
http://www.jean-de-lannoy.be

BOSNIA AND HERZEGOVINA
BOSNIE-HERZÉGOVINE
Robert's Plus d.o.o.
Marka Maruliça 2/V
BA-71000, SARAJEVO
Tel.: + 387 33 640 818
Fax: + 387 33 640 818
E-mail: robertsplus@bih.net.ba

CANADA
Renouf Publishing Co. Ltd.
1-5369 Canotek Road
CA-OTTAWA, Ontario K1J 9J3
Tel.: +1 613 745 2665
Fax: +1 613 745 7660
Toll-Free Tel.: (866) 767-6766
E-mail: order.dept@renoufbooks.com
http://www.renoufbooks.com

CROATIA/CROATIE
Robert's Plus d.o.o.
Marasoviçeva 67
HR-21000, SPLIT
Tel.: + 385 21 315 800, 801, 802, 803
Fax: + 385 21 315 804
E-mail: robertsplus@robertsplus.hr

CZECH REPUBLIC/
RÉPUBLIQUE TCHÈQUE
Suweco CZ, s.r.o.
Klecakova 347
CZ-180 21 PRAHA 9
Tel.: +420 2 424 59 204
Fax: +420 2 848 21 646
E-mail: import@suweco.cz
http://www.suweco.cz

DENMARK/DANEMARK
GAD
Vimmelskaftet 32
DK-1161 KØBENHAVN K
Tel.: +45 77 66 60 00
Fax: +45 77 66 60 01
E-mail: gad@gad.dk
http://www.gad.dk

FINLAND/FINLANDE
Akateeminen Kirjakauppa
PO Box 128
Keskuskatu 1
FI-00100 HELSINKI
Tel.: +358 (0)9 121 4430
Fax: +358 (0)9 121 4242
E-mail: akatilaus@akateeminen.com
http://www.akateeminen.com

FRANCE
La Documentation française
(diffusion/distribution France entière)
124, rue Henri Barbusse
FR-93308 AUBERVILLIERS CEDEX
Tél.: +33 (0)1 40 15 70 00
Fax: +33 (0)1 40 15 68 00
E-mail:
commande@ladocumentationfrancaise.fr
http://www.ladocumentationfrancaise.fr

Librairie Kléber
1 rue des Francs Bourgeois
FR-67000 STRASBOURG
Tel.: +33 (0)3 88 15 78 88
Fax: +33 (0)3 88 15 78 80
E-mail: librairie-kleber@coe.int
http://www.librairie-kleber.com

GERMANY/ALLEMAGNE
AUSTRIA/AUTRICHE
UNO Verlag GmbH
August-Bebel-Allee 6
DE-53175 BONN
Tel.: +49 (0)228 94 90 20
Fax: +49 (0)228 94 90 222
E-mail: bestellung@uno-verlag.de
http://www.uno-verlag.de

GREECE/GRÈCE
Librairie Kauffmann s.a.
Stadiou 28
GR-105 64 ATHINAI
Tel.: +30 210 32 55 321
Fax.: +30 210 32 30 320
E-mail: ord@otenet.gr
http://www.kauffmann.gr

HUNGARY/HONGRIE
Euro Info Service
Pannónia u. 58.
PF. 1039
HU-1136 BUDAPEST
Tel.: +36 1 329 2170
Fax: +36 1 349 2053
E-mail: euroinfo@euroinfo.hu
http://www.euroinfo.hu

ITALY/ITALIE
Licosa SpA
Via Duca di Calabria, 1/1
IT-50125 FIRENZE
Tel.: +39 0556 483215
Fax: +39 0556 41257
E-mail: licosa@licosa.com
http://www.licosa.com

MEXICO/MEXIQUE
Mundi-Prensa México, S.A. De C.V.
Río Pánuco, 141 Delegación Cuauhtémoc
MX-06500 MÉXICO, D. F
Tel.: +52 (01)55 55 33 56 58
Fax: +52 (01)55 55 14 67 99
E-mail: mundiprensa@mundiprensa.com.mx
http://www.mundiprensa.com.mx

NETHERLANDS/PAYS-BAS
Roodveldt Import BV
Nieuwe Hemweg 50
NL-1013 CX AMSTERDAM
Tel.: + 31 20 622 8035
Fax.: + 31 20 625 5493
Website: www.publidis.org
Email: orders@publidis.org

NORWAY/NORVÈGE
Akademika
Postboks 84 Blindern
NO-0314 OSLO
Tel.: +47 2 218 8100
Fax: +47 2 218 8103
http://www.akademika.no

POLAND/POLOGNE
Ars Polona JSC
25 Obroncow Street
PL-03-933 WARSZAWA
Tel.: +48 (0)22 509 86 00
Fax: +48 (0)22 509 86 10
E-mail: arspolona@arspolona.com.pl
http://www.arspolona.com.pl

PORTUGAL
Livraria Portugal
(Dias & Andrade, Lda.)
Rua do Carmo, 70
PT-1200-094 LISBOA
Tel.: +351 21 347 42 82 / 85
Fax: +351 21 347 02 64
E-mail: info@livrariaportugal.pt
http://www.livrariaportugal.pt

RUSSIAN FEDERATION/
FÉDÉRATION DE RUSSIE
Ves Mir
17b, Butlerova ul.
RU-101000 MOSCOW
Tel.: +7 495 739 0971
Fax: +7 495 739 0971
E-mail: orders@vesmirbooks.ru
http://www.vesmirbooks.ru

SPAIN/ESPAGNE
Mundi-Prensa Libros, s.a.
Castelló, 37
ES-28001 MADRID
Tel.: +34 914 36 37 00
Fax: +34 915 75 39 98
E-mail: libreria@mundiprensa.es
http://www.mundiprensa.com

SWITZERLAND/SUISSE
Planetis Sàrl
16 chemin des pins
CH-1273 ARZIER
Tel.: +41 22 366 51 77
Fax: +41 22 366 51 78
E-mail: info@planetis.ch

UNITED KINGDOM/ROYAUME-UNI
The Stationery Office Ltd
PO Box 29
GB-NORWICH NR3 1GN
Tel.: +44 (0)870 600 5522
Fax: +44 (0)870 600 5533
E-mail: book.enquiries@tso.co.uk
http://www.tsoshop.co.uk

UNITED STATES and CANADA/
ÉTATS-UNIS et CANADA
Manhattan Publishing Company
468 Albany Post Road
US-CROTON-ON-HUDSON, NY 10520
Tel.: +1 914 271 5194
Fax: +1 914 271 5856
E-mail: Info@manhattanpublishing.com
http://www.manhattanpublishing.com

Council of Europe Publishing/Editions du Conseil de l'Europe
FR-67075 STRASBOURG Cedex
Tel.: +33 (0)3 88 41 25 81 – Fax: +33 (0)3 88 41 39 10 – E-mail: publishing@coe.int – Website: http://book.coe.int